JAPANESE COOKING NOW

Honorable husband make beautiful
Japanese Garden for wife,
Good Japanese wife make beautiful
food for honorable husband.
Rattow Ruck

Love

Mary & Roland

Also by Joan Itoh
Rice-Paddy Gourmet

JAPANESE COOKING NOW

by Joan Itoh
Illustrations by Tadashi Ohashi

WARNER BOOKS

Warner Books, Inc., 75 Rockefeller Plaza, New York, N.Y. 10019

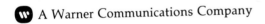 A Warner Communications Company

Printed and bound in Japan
First Printing: May 1980
10 9 8 7 6 5 4 3 2 1

Library of Congress Cataloging in Publication Data

Itoh, Joan.
   Japanese cooking now.

   Includes index.
   1. Cookery, Japanese.   I. Title.
TX724.5.J318   641.5′952   79-17431
ISBN 0-446-51206-0

Table of Contents

Introduction

When I went to live in Japan I knew, like most Americans in 1965, precious little about Japanese food. Living in the Japanese countryside as part of a Japanese family was a big adventure, and food was very much a part of that adventure. When I took my first trip home in 1972, it therefore came as quite a surprise to find bean curd, soybean sprouts and other everyday Japanese foodstuffs available in many American supermarkets.

In recent years, Americans have become more and more aware of the caloric and nutritional value of the foods they are eating. Expressions such as "junk foods" and "empty calories" have come into our language, and health-food stores and restaurants have popped up in many cities across the U.S.A.

Concerned with obesity, heart attacks and breast cancer, people began looking to the eating habits of the Orient where these problems are just not that prevalent. The average Japanese may know and care nothing for the calories in his diet, but the average Japanese is not fat. Perhaps it is for different reasons, but less fatty foods became more desirable in the West too, and soybean products, with their inexpensive high protein value, excited a lot of interest. It became apparent to many that it made good sense to learn about and to acquire a taste for the natural foods eaten in Japan.

American women's magazines began to print articles to this effect and a very exclusive health farm, where wealthy American women go to get into shape, started to fashion its menus from the Japanese cuisine. People found that Japanese food is not only healthy but delicious, with a different range of delicate flavors. It is unique in many ways, especially in the aesthetic appeal of its presentation. A lot of artistic expression can go into arranging Japanese dishes. In Japan, it is not unusual to find the vegetables sculpted into lovely flower shapes, for instance. The volume of each dish is small but the food can be highly satisfying because much attention is paid to the colors and textures of the combinations in a meal. A well-prepared Japanese meal can give pleasure to more senses than just the taste buds.

The absolute freshness of the vegetables and fish is all part of this highly aesthetic approach to food. The Japanese eat with the seasons and the "first of the season," of whatever it may be, is greatly prized. Every Japanese looks forward to tasting the first bamboo shoots, the first eggplants, mushrooms, or whatever, when they first appear on the market during the year. The first rice is especially enjoyed. This is a joy that we of the frozen-food cultures have forgotten.

Because the Japanese have a totally different approach to food from that of Westerners, Japanese dishes don't easily fit into the usual Western cookbook format. Because of this, instead of classifying the recipes under fish, meat, vegetables, etc., in this book I classify the foods in the order in which the various dishes are ordinarily served in the Japanese home.

There are no set menus for a Japanese meal but there is a certain kind of order. Except for formal dinners, foods from all the following categories are not always served together in the Japanese home; rather, the average cook chooses dishes from a few of the categories below:

1 *Zensai* (hors-d'oeuvre)
2 *Sashimi* (sliced raw fish)
3 *Yakimono* (broiled or grilled foods)
4 *Nimono* (boiled foods)
5 *Mushimono* (steamed dishes)
6 *Sunomono* and *aemono* (salads and dressed foods)
7 *Agemono* (fried foods)
8 *Nabemono* (cooked at the table)
9 *Tsukemono* (pickles)
10 *Misoshiru* (thick soups) and *Suimono* (clear soups)
11 *Gohan* (rice dishes)
12 *Menrui* (noodles—*soba* and *udon*)
13 *Kudamono* (fruit)
14 *Nominomo* (beverages)

Explanations

If you have never been to Japan, the chances are you are going to find many of the ingredients in Japanese recipes rather exotic and unfamiliar. I had this problem at first but it didn't take long to be at home with them and to appreciate the various different flavors and textures, as the Japanese do. Of course living in the Japanese countryside helped a lot. Just as one has to know something about a culture in order to learn and appreciate a foreign language, one also has to know something about a culture to like and appreciate its food. For this reason, these explanations are going to be spiced with little bits and pieces of what I know and feel about these foods and maybe that will help you to enjoy cooking and eating them as much as I do.

Seaweeds   Maybe you have never eaten seaweed in your life and you may feel this food to be very strange, yet the sea certainly isn't all that strange to you. Most of us have spent time near the ocean sometime in our lives and we know the feel of the waters, the sounds of the waves and the smell of the fresh salty air. We know there is a whole different world existing in those huge masses of water but we also know that it is still very much a part of our earth.

The Japanese as a people are more intimate with the sea than most Americans are. Their small country is a sprinkling of islands in the midst of a vast ocean. Almost no place in Japan is very far from the sea and, lacking the land to yield enough food for their people, the Japanese learned a long time ago to take much of their food from the world under the water. Seaweeds are just the wild plants that grow in the underwater fields and their taste isn't much different from the good, fresh ocean air.

Developing a taste for seaweed and learning how to use it as a food is well worth the effort. It is a health food of the first order and makes lovely stocks and sauces. It gives our bodies all sorts of minerals such as iodine, iron, calcium, potassium, magnesium and phosphorus, and vitamins A, B^2 and niacin. The Japanese people also believe that eating seaweed makes one's hair thick, black and healthy.

The three most commonly eaten varieties of seaweed in Japan are *nori, wakame* and *konbu. Nori* is probably the most popular; it is sold in a form that looks like greenish-black sheets of paper. These seaweed "papers" are usually about eight inches square. The sheets are held over a fire and toasted. When they are crisp enough, they are usually crumbled or cut into thin strips and used as a garnish for foods. Vinegared rice and other ingredients are often rolled in this seaweed to make *nori-maki,* a kind of rolled rice sandwich. All kinds of pretoasted, uniformly cut pieces of *nori* are sold in packages inside airtight tins and are a must for every Japanese household. Japanese people like to dip a piece into soy sauce and eat this with a mouthful of rice. This is very often part of a typical Japanese breakfast.

Wakame is a long curly seaweed that is generally sold fresh, sprinkled with salt. It is rinsed in cold water before using and it is found in soups, salads and many other Japanese dishes. Various areas in Japan are said to have more tasty *wakame* than others and people who visit these places will often bring back some for their friends and relatives. The Japanese love to travel and they like to let others know when they have had a chance to leave their hometowns. When the gift of food from another part of Japan is served, along with it will undoubtedly go the news and stories of the gift-giver's trip. In the case of seaweed or dried fish, a Tokyo household may enjoy a gift from someone who visited, say, the Sea of Japan. Along with the taste will go the feeling of the colder, rougher waters that beat against the shores of the other side of their island country. *Wakame* is a great favorite to go into the *miso* soup that Japanese people love and often have every day.

Konbu is dried kelp and is sold in many varieties. Whenever I think of a Japanese fishing village, I think of the beaches where women spread out the kelp on low wooden frames to dry in the sun. One of these varieties of kelp is *konbu,* the long pieces of dried seaweed that are washed, soaked to soften them, and often slit to let out the good flavor. From this *dashi-konbu* comes the stock *dashi* with which so many Japanese dishes are made. *Dashi* stock is the backbone of Japanese cuisine.

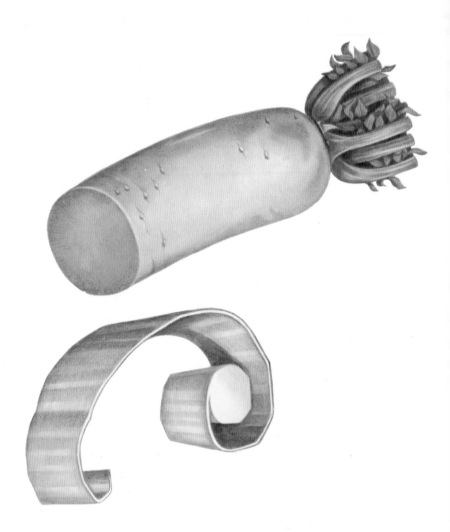

Daikon (Japanese Radish)
A super large, white radish that is beginning to make its well-deserved appearance in Western supermarkets. *Daikon* means "large" or "great root" in Japanese and it probably is one of the world's largest radishes since it can grow up to two feet or more in length. It is also a rich source of vitamin C and, despite its size, has a delicate flavor. When cooked it can taste like a white radish and when eaten raw it tastes something like an icicle radish. If it is not available, then either one of these other radishes may substitute. The skilled Japanese cook cuts the *daikon* paper-thin for edible garnishes or grates it fresh just before serving *tempura* sauce, or other dipping sauces. It is also served freshly grated for *sunomono* or Japanese-type salads. And it is cooked in stews and soups and made into the pickles that are eaten almost every day in Japan.

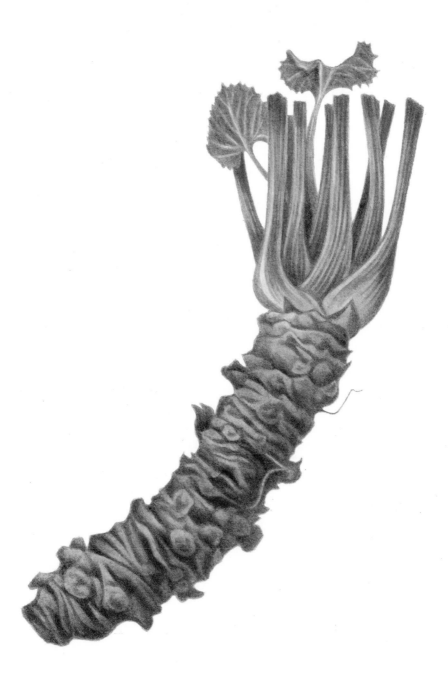

Wasabi (Horseradish)

The best Japanese horseradish is fresh *wasabi,* sold commonly in Japan but rarely in the U.S.A. When grated, it is a hot-tasting bright-green substance that gives a bit of zip to some Japanese foods. The white horseradish that Americans are fond of putting on their roast beef is just not the same thing. However, *wasabi* can be bought in a dried form and is available in stores that sell Oriental foods. Put a little of the green powder in a small cup, add a few drops of water, and turn the cup upside down. In a few minutes you will have the same horseradish used in Japan, but use it sparingly because it is really hot stuff.

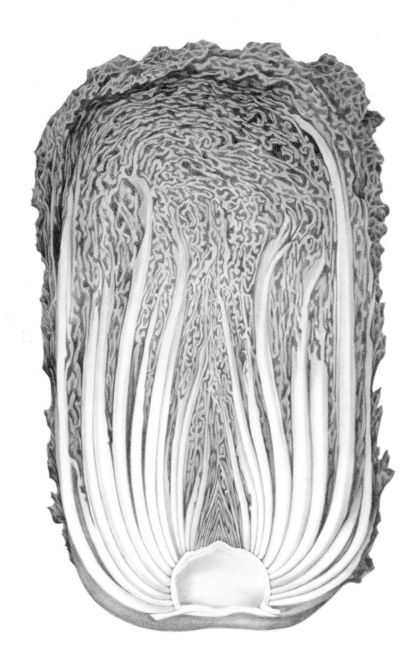

Hakusai (Chinese Cabbage)

This is a very close relative to our Chinese cabbage (called *bok choy* in Chinese), also called celery cabbage by some. A long, almost white-leaved cabbage, it is milder in taste than ordinary cabbage. In Japan it is inexpensive and available everywhere. The Chinese cabbage we have in the West does very well for the recipes here that call for *hakusai* and it is also ideal for use in Western salads and other dishes that call for raw greens. *Hakusai* is a favorite for the *nabe* dishes cooked at the table in Japan, as well as for stews and soups. Every Japanese housewife often makes salted *hakusai* pickles which are eaten along with boiled rice at the end of a Japanese meal.

8

Shōga (Ginger)

One of the joys of living in the Orient is the availability of fresh *shoga,* or gingerroot. A boon to any cook, the peeled, grated or chopped gingerroot can put zest into anything from sauces to saké. Small pieces of fresh gingerroot are often served along with grilled fish, and *sushi* wouldn't be *sushi* without a generous helping of the delicious sweet-and-sour ginger pickles. Fresh gingerroot and several kinds of ginger pickles are often available in Oriental food shops in the West but ground ginger is available almost anywhere. It does not have quite the same flavor as freshly grated gingerroot but it will serve well for the recipes in this book.

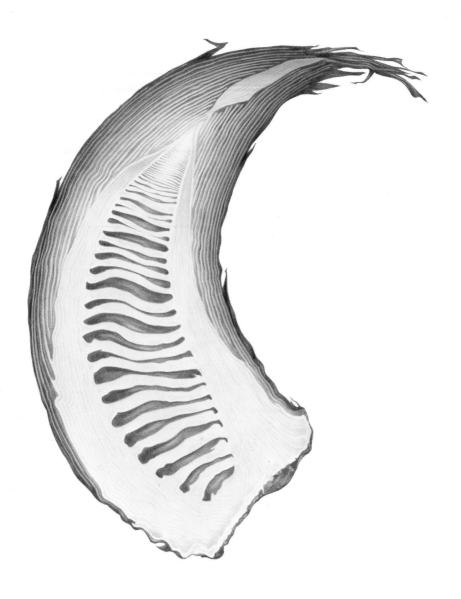

Takenoko (Bamboo Shoot)

The fresh, young tender shoots of the Japanese variety of bamboo are a taste treat usually enjoyed in Japan only in early spring. A slightly different tasting but good bamboo shoot is available other times of the year and this is peeled, cooked and sold in little plastic bags. In the West, we mostly know the less tender Chinese variety of bamboo shoots which are sometimes available fresh, but mostly canned, and are sold in the Oriental food section of many supermarkets. This is more convenient for the Western cook, as bamboo shoots are troublesome to husk and require long cooking. The canned variety can be used nicely in Japanese recipes but it is advised first to rinse them well under cold water to reduce the taste of salt that is sometimes added when canning. Bamboo, a popular low-calorie vegetable, was first canned in the city of Wakayama in Japan back in 1880.

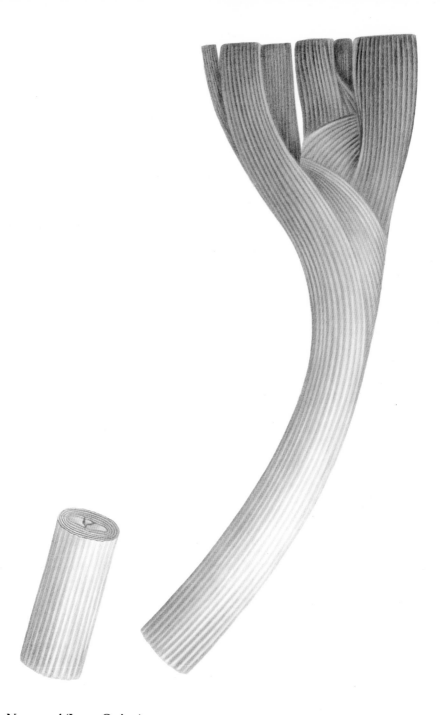

Naganegi (Long Onion)

A long onion, very long by Western standards, and very mild. It is not as sweet as some of our round onions are and not as pungent as chives are. Nor has it the strong taste of our ordinary cooking onion. When thinly sliced, *naganegi* is perfect for a garnish and is used in sauces, soups and salads. Some of the mild varieties of Western onions might be used in place of *naganegi* but the Japanese long onions are now being grown in the West and are seen more and more in Western supermarkets and greengrocery shops.

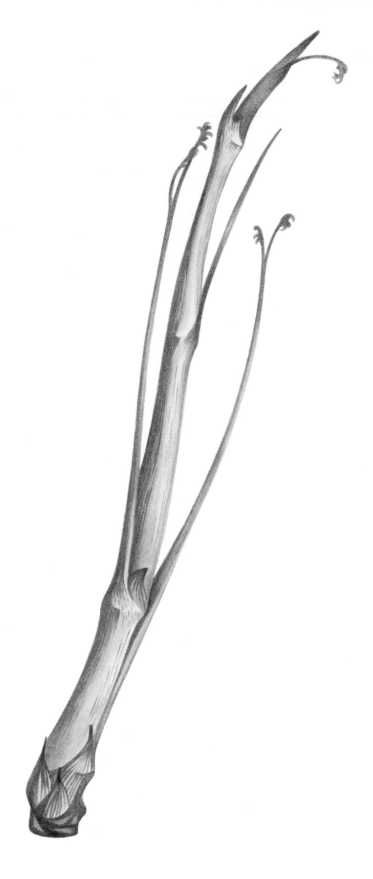

Udo

The nearest thing the West has to this delicate vegetable is spikenard, a plant akin to valerian which was once used to make aromatic ointment. *Udo* in taste somewhat resembles celery but is much milder. The Japanese raise it, like mushrooms, without sunlight and so it comes to the table very white, soft and delicate. If you are using celery in its place, make sure all string membrane is removed and don't add any of the strong-tasting leaves. *Udo* can be added to salads and many other recipes. When used in soups, add just before serving.

Sazae (Turbo)

This is the turbo, or wreath shell, which is found many places in the world, but commonly eaten mainly in Japan—another example of how the Japanese enjoy eating many foods, especially seafoods, that many other people shun. It is usually prepared in its own shell and is a treat that everyone seems to expect and enjoy at Japanese beach parties. It is especially good when roasted over an open fire but is also very good when prepared at home in the oven.

Hasu (Lotus Root)

Lotus root is not easy to find a substitute for because of its unique, delicate flavor and its wonderfully crisp texture. It is also a beautiful vegetable when sliced crosswise because of the patterns formed by the hollow spaces that run the length of each root. Fresh lotus root is not easily found in Western food stores but canned lotus root is available where Oriental foods are sold and retains much of the delicious flavor. It is an excellent addition to many dishes; thinly sliced lotus root marinated in sweetened vinegar makes a very special refrigerator pickle.

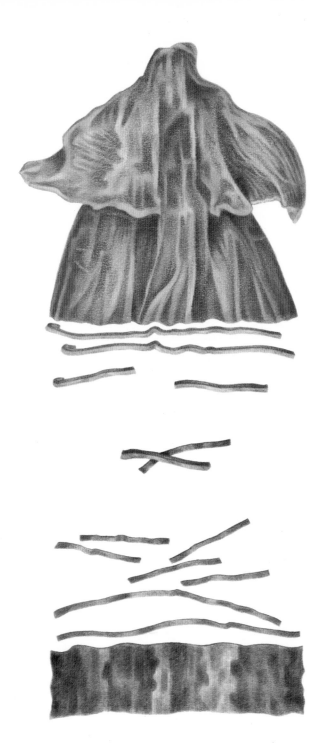

Ika (Squid)
Squid is a popular food in Japan, as the waters around Japan abound with it. The Japanese are fond of eating raw squid as well as cooking it in various sauces. Almost all over Japan one can see squid drying in the sun on the beaches, and dried squid is used in a variety of ways. Cut crosswise into thin pieces (as illustrated), it is a snack food enjoyed anytime and anywhere, especially with beer or saké.

Matsutake (Pine Mushroom)
Pine mushrooms are a real gourmet treat in Japan; they are sold only in the autumn and then only at an enormous price. They grow under the red pine trees in the mountains and are difficult to gather. They can have a cap up to half a foot across but are considered the best before the cap is opened. Other mushrooms can be substituted in recipes calling for *matsutake* but of course the flavor won't be exactly the same. Every Japanese looks forward to eating *matsutake gohan,* rice made with pine mushrooms, in the autumn of the year. Sometimes *matsutake* are available in the northwest areas of the United States but many people have no idea how good they are.

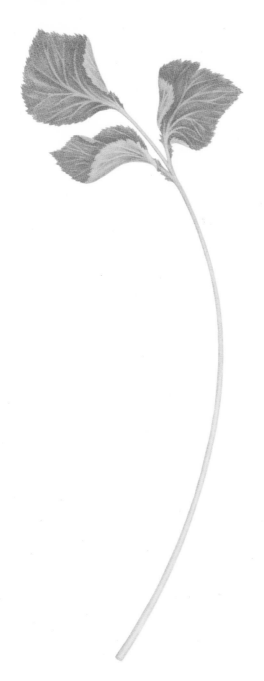

Mitsuba (Trefoie)

We have nothing like this delicate and pungent plant, the stalks and leaves of which offer one of Japan's most pleasant and typical tastes. *Mitsuba* is a watery plant and its porous stalk is a bit like that of the nasturtium. The Western plant which most closely resembles it is probably the watercress, though its taste is much stronger. *Mitsuba* is used in a number of ways. One finds it in various *suimono* and in some varieties of *misoshiru* as well. It is also found in *aemono* and other saladlike dishes. Only the fresh, young shoots and leaves are eaten. The mature plant loses its subtle but typical taste.

Kabocha (**Pumpkin Squash**)
The Japanese pumpkin squash looks like a small American pumpkin with a dark-green skin. The flavor is rich. *Kabocha* is available all over Japan during most seasons. Because it was one of the foods that most people ate during the lean war years, Japanese of that generation are not overly fond of it, but it is still widely used in many dishes by thrifty Japanese house-wives—a favorite in mixtures boiled in sauces, fried *tempura* style, or added to stews or soups. Winter squash or pumpkin is very similar in flavor and texture.

Nasu (Eggplant)

Eggplants, or aubergines, in Japan are usually a smaller and much more tender variety than that commonly found in the West. The flavor of these tiny eggplants is prized in the early autumn. A test of a good Japanese cook is how good in both flavor and color her eggplant pickles are. Now, of course, the larger eggplant are availabe in Japan and the housewives make delicious dishes from them too, but the small ones are still preferred. Small eggplants, like pine mushrooms, have long been favorite subjects for works of art in Japan.

Kuri (Chestnut) and *Ginnan* (Ginkgo)

Chestnuts and ginkgo are often used in Japanese recipes. The chestnuts are much like our Western chestnuts; they are often sweetened with sugar. The ginkgo nut is just beginning to be seen in Western supermarkets and people are beginning to realize how good they can be roasted just as chestnuts are roasted. Fresh or canned ginkgo nuts are also used in soups and *nabe* cooking, or served on skewers. They have a delicate flavor and are usually liked by Westerners as well as by Asians.

Irori or *Jizaikagi*

This is the Japanese answer to the Western fireplace and it is still found in some old farmhouses around Japan. It was rarely found in the home of a samurai or lord as it was considered common to have fire in the house, but the ordinary folk found great comfort in their firepit. It was a place fashioned in a shallow pit in the floor where a fire was made on a bed of ash. It was used for warmth and cooking and much of Japanese family life took place around the *irori*. A bamboo pole hung from the ceiling and on it was a hook to hold a large pot or kettle. Very often a wooden carving, usually of a fish, decorated the bottom of the bamboo pole.

The kettle that hung over the *irori* boiled the water for the count-less cups of tea required in a Japanese home. The large pots cooked stews, soups and *nabe* meals for chilly days. The smoke from the fire darkened and aged the woods in the house and the fish and gourds hung from a frame over the fire to dry. To experience a meal from the pot over the fire in the *irori* is to experience the Japan of old.

Dashi   Here is a Japanese word you will become familiar with when you start doing any kind of Japanese cooking. Even the most basic Japanese dishes may call for a clear liquid stock and this is called *dashi.*

The most common *dashi* made by the Japanese is made from *dashi-konbu,* the seaweed I was talking about, and *katsuo-bushi.* If you don't live in Japan, no one will expect you to remember the name *katsuo-bushi* and you are probably thankful for that. You can just call it a dried bonito fillet because that is exactly what it is. Boned, these bonito fillets are very slowly dried until they look like fish fashioned out of old wood. They sometimes have a bit of a greenish color which is supposed to add to their flavor. So the rule for *katsuo-bushi* is that the more antique it looks, the better the *dashi* it will make.

Of course, all this is just for your information because, like so many things in Japan these days, *dashi* is now bought commonly in little "instant" packages. As a matter of fact, there are probably a great many of the Japanese younger generation who don't know what a dried bonito fillet looks like, but I'm sorry for them because *dashi* made from *katsuo-bushi* is so much better.

So, just in case you happen to be old-fashioned like me, and want to make your *dashi* from scratch, let me tell you about one thing you will need besides the dried fish. This is a *kezuri-bako.* This may sound exotic but it is just a wooden box equipped with a razor set in the top. The box has a drawer-like compartment in the bottom. You rub the dried bonito on the razor and the shavings fall into the drawer. That is all there is to it and it is the bonito shavings and the *konbu* that make the real thing.

Basic *Dashi*

1 piece of *dashi-konbu* about 4 inches long
1 ounce *katsuo-bushi* shavings, approximately
5 cups water

Wipe the *konbu* with a damp cloth. Cut several slits in it with a clean scissors. The flavor will steep out of these cuts into the soup. Place the *konbu* in the water and heat. Just before the water boils, take *konbu* out. It has done its work, so you can throw it away. Add a little cold water to keep the broth from boiling immediately. Add the *katsuo-bushi* shavings. When the broth begins to boil, turn off the heat. The secret is not to let the broth boil.

After the shavings sink to the bottom, spoon the broth off the top and strain it. Carelessly pouring the broth through a strainer results in a cloudy soup, so do it carefully. Makes about 4 cups.

For those who like to do things the easy way, the same market that sells dried bonito fillets will surely have instant *dashi,* often called *dashi-no-moto.* The little foil packages will hold the right amount for one recipe and probably only a good Japanese grandmother could tell the difference.

For variety, or in case of unavailability, you can use other dried fish for your basic *dashi.* Dried bonito is not inexpensive and I have been in many a Japanese kitchen that made its *dashi* with less expensive dried young sardines. To do this, the sardines are put into cold water, left to stand overnight and then boiled for 3 to 5 minutes. The stock is ready when strained well.

However, if the taste of the sea is not exactly your favorite flavor, you might prefer to do your Japanese cooking with chicken stock. Any recipe calling for basic *dashi* can be made with chicken stock. If you want it to be authentic *dashi,* you can make your chicken stock the Japanese way.

Japanese Chicken *Dashi*

1 pound chicken bones, approximately
1 teaspoon vinegar
2 long onions
2 small pieces of gingerroot, crushed (optional)
8 cups water

Put all the ingredients in a pan. Bring to a boil, skimming from time to time to remove excess fat. The vinegar softens the bones and though it doesn't really add much to the taste it does get more flavor out of the bones. Simmer gently to reduce the liquid by half. Strain carefully. Makes about 4 cups.

Gohan   No one can talk about the basic parts of the Japanese meal, or even about Japan for that matter, without talking about rice. Cooked rice is called *gohan* in Japanese and very often the entire meal is also called *gohan.*

Maybe it is because I lived in the Japanese countryside but I certainly think of Japan as a rice-culture. So much of life there revolves around the planting, tending, harvesting and eating of rice. It was a surprise to me that many a farmer brought the rice seeds into his home to coax them into sprouting when the planting season began. The seeds are usually soaked outdoors, but I have seen great sacks of rice seeds sitting in the warm water of the wooden family bath. Perhaps this is only done in the cold climates but seeing it done this way in Niigata impressed me very much. The rice seemed even a more intimate part of the Japanese farmer's life, having stayed awhile developing under his roof and protection.

When the seeds begin to crack, they are planted close to each other in a field and tended lovingly until they have sprouted to the height of the farmer's fist. They are then planted, one at a time, well spaced and even today, often by hand. No wonder many Japanese have a great respect for rice. It represents so much work and concern and so many bent backs.

It has been really interesting for me to watch the old people—especially those who have spent their lives in the rice fields—when they eat the fruit of their labors. There is no doubt that these old folks handle rice with the greatest care and would never waste any. I have seen them pick up with their chopsticks every grain from the top of their lunchbox before they start on the actual lunch. When beginning their meal, they hold the bowl in both hands and make a little bow, lifting it in a gesture of thanks before starting. They eat every grain in their bowls and usually fill the bowl with tea, drinking down the last clinging flavor of the rice. I come from a culture where fresh-baked bread is a wonderful treat, but it is amazing that any one food can be so important to a people as *gohan* is to the Japanese.

The Japanese have a very different idea from Westerners about what good rice should look and taste like. You might pride yourself on cooking fluffy rice with the grains almost separated, but this would never be considered desirable in Japan. Japanese rice is stickier, perhaps because it is eaten with chopsticks, but it still must be fluffy. Japanese rice is also a shorter grain than most Westerners like, but it is close to California rice both in looks and in flavor.

To cook rice like a Japanese takes a little experimenting. Most Japanese cooks don't bother to measure, as they have been seeing rice prepared all their lives. For the beginner, however, it is safe to allow 1¼ cups of water for every cup of rice.

Basic Rice

5 cups rice
6 cups cold water
(California Rose or round-grain rice is closest to the
   Japanese variety.)

Rinse rice well under cold tap water. Drain and put into a heavy pot. Add cold water. Let it stand for at least 30 minutes. Boil over high heat until water bubbles; then turn the heat down so the water doesn't boil over. Cook for 10 minutes. Turn the heat to low and cook for another 15 minutes. Turn off heat completely but let the pan stand for 10 to 15 minutes before removing the cover. This is very important for good rice. Never take the lid off the pan while the rice is cooking. The loss of steam affects the cooking process. Always let the rice rest for at least 10 minutes after cooking without removing the lid. Before serving, fluff up rice with a large spoon. In Japan this is done with a *shamoji,* or wooden spatula. Makes 6 servings.

Soybeans and Soybean Products   Ah, the noble soybean! It has long been the pillar of protein in the Japanese diet and this vegetable protein has served them well. Traditionally, Japan has not been a meat-eating country and it was mainly through soybeans and the many products made from soybeans that the average Japanese got the protein so needed for good health. Americans, on the other hand, feed soybeans to animals, but actually the amount of usable protein contained in just half a cup of inexpensive soybeans is not much different from that contained in five ounces of very expensive steak.

What may be more important is that soybean products contain no cholesterol and are low in calories compared to other high-protein foods. It is no wonder that the West is beginning to change its mind about soybeans. Most people know now that more can be made from soybeans than just soy sauce.

Miso   This is fermented soybean paste. You may have heard about it but you may not know that it is a basic staple food in Japan. It is used for making soups that are part of the everyday Japanese diet. It is used to make sauces and also for pickling meat and fish.

Miso comes in many types and varieties and actually varies in flavor from region to region in Japan. There is the so-called white, sweet *miso* that is made in the Kyoto area, a mellow yellow type that comes from Kyushu and a red salty type that is usually associated with the northern colder areas.

In Niigata, the area where I lived in Japan, May was the month for making *miso.* I remember this clearly because it was wisteria time and the purple and white flowers hung down over a small pond in the back of our house and the petals often floated on the water over brilliantly colored fish.

Past the pond was an old barnlike structure that was used only once a year for making *miso.* It housed a large old cooking stove, a remnant of days gone by, but the local farmers still came and had a community *miso*-making project every year. A very important project it was too because the farmers I knew in Niigata had *miso* soup two or three times a day.

Like so many other things in Japan, *miso* came from China through Korea, in about the eighth century. The Japanese didn't know much about fermentation back then so it was not food for the average citizen. It wasn't until the 1500s that it began to be popular. The samurai found it a very convenient food for the battlefield and the demand for *miso* grew.

About 70 percent of all the *miso* made in Japan is made from a combination of soybeans and rice, steamed and crushed together; 20 percent is made from soybeans and wheat and only about 10 percent is made from pure soybeans.

Tofu   This is no stranger to health-food fans in the West. It is a curd made from the soybean and it too comes in a great many forms and shapes. Since this is a book about contemporary Japanese cooking, let's just get into the three most popular varieties of *tofu,* keeping in mind, however, there are many more.

You should know these three. Plain *tofu, yaki-dofu* and *abura-age.* Plain *tofu* is sold in what looks like a small white block of well-formed custard. This usually weighs about 10 ounces. *Yaki-dofu* is basically the same thing but it comes in a smaller square. Its outside is nicely browned from grilling and the curd doesn't contain quite so much liquid. *Abura-age,* which comes in thin flat rectangles, is even firmer and browner, as it is deep-fried *tofu.*

Shoyu   This is soy sauce, perhaps the best known of the soybean products. Oriental foods are just not Oriental foods without it. The Japanese use it on almost everything in small or big quantities. It is made from wheat and soybeans, mixed with malt seed and allowed to ferment. Japanese *shoyu* and Chinese soy sauce often differ a bit in flavor and texture. I am going to insist that you make the recipes in this book with Japanese *shoyu* and not Chinese soy sauce, or you will just not get the desired results. The excellence of Chinese food, like that of French food, has a lot to do with the sauces they are so fond of. Not true in the same sense in Japan. The excellence of Japanese food is in the delicate natural tastes of the foods themselves. This may not be completely true in their homey country cooking but in sophisticated places like the old capital of Kyoto, all their flavoring, including *miso* and *shoyu,* is very light. Real Japanese *shoyu,* which is lighter than Chinese soy sauce, is available just about everywhere these days. Perhaps the most popular one goes under the brand name of Kikkoman.

Goma (Sesame)   It may seem rather imprudent to get excited over a seed but I have been a sesame-seed fan from way back. I used to make my own rolls and breads in the U.S. because the ones at the local bakery never had enough sesame seeds on them for my taste. It was therefore a delightful surprise to find that so many Japanese recipes were made with sesame seeds, called *goma* in Japan. Not only that, but oil of sesame is commonly used for cooking in Japan and I could happily indulge in an absolute flavor favorite.

Sesame seeds come in both black and white varieties in Japan and are sold everywhere, even in the smallest of mountain villages. They require parching when used in Japanese cooking and can easily be prepared by dry-frying them in a hot, heavy skillet until they begin to jump. They are then usually ground in a mortar but one American friend of mine simply pops them into her electric coffee grinder and it works beautifully.

***Su* (Vinegar)**   A word about vinegar is called for here because there are many kinds of vinegars in the West and many are not suitable for Japanese recipes. Wine and fruit vinegars are too heavy but there are several light, white vinegars available in the U.S.A. that come close to Japanese vinegar, which is a rice vinegar. Heinz distilled vinegar should do nicely.

***Kamaboko* (Fish Paste)**   The Japanese people eat a lot of fish paste and there is a tremendous assortment of it on the Japanese market. In the U.S.A. it is usually only sold in stores that sell Oriental foods but I have also seen it in supermarkets in California. That is probably because there are many Japanese living there.

Without living in Japan, it is very difficult to picture or understand the different kinds of fish paste but a few words on the subject should prepare you for some of the recipes in this book. The fish cake that these recipes call for is mostly *kamaboko*. Two other common types in Japan are *chikuwa* and *hanpen*. All of these are made primarily of white fish, mostly cod and shark.

Shark may be a surprise to you but, why not?—it's protein. The fish is washed, all blood, bone and fat is removed, and then it is ground down into a paste and cooked. The result is not terribly high in calories, but it is a good source of protein and very inexpensive. The taste? Rather mild and most people like it though it may need a bit of doctoring for some.

Just as a bit of information, the oldest known of these

fish paste products is *chikuwa,* though it was called *kamaboko* back in the thirteenth century. Yet it was very similar to that which is called *chikuwa* today. That may sound very confusing but *chikuwa* means bamboo ring; in those ancient days, the paste was patted around a bamboo shaft and cooked over a fire. When it was taken off the bamboo, its long tubelike shape reminded people of the head of a bullrush. Bullrush in Japanese is *gama no ho* and this came to be pronounced *kamaboko.*

In the Edo Period (which ended well over one hundred years ago) a new shape was made for this steamed fish. This is the loaflike one that is now popular today and that too was called *kamaboko.* Finally someone decided to rename the tube-shape fish paste, so they went back to calling it *chikuwa,* meaning bamboo ring.

The most recent addition to the fish paste family is called *hanpen.* This is basically the same ground white fish mixed with *yamaimo* (mountain potato). The consistency is different, softer, and it usually comes in a rectangular shape.

Fu *Fu,* a food that looks like bread, is made of wheat gluten and comes in many shapes and forms. It is not always easy to find outside of Japan so just a few recipes in this book call for it. However, if you can find it at your Oriental food store, get acquainted with it as it is good for you and tastes very nice.

There are four most common types of *fu: Arare,* or "hail," *fu.* It is shaped like little light balls and is very good in soups. There is *hana,* or "flower," *fu* and it looks like small flowers and is very decorative in clear soups. The most common is *kuruma,* or "wheel," *fu.* It looks like a cross between French bread and a Jewish bagel. You can buy it in nice neat packages all over Japan but one often sees this *fu* hung from the ceiling in small country stores. This is good in soup and in *nimono* (boiled dishes). Perhaps *shona fu* is the one that is most likely to be found outside Japan. I have seen this in supermarkets in California. It is a long flat cracker type and very good in *miso* soup.

Mirin This is an extrasweet kind of saké, used mainly for cooking. Though saké itself, like other wines, comes both dry and sweet, *mirin* is quite different. It is supersweet and a little goes a long way. Yet, it is widely used and Japanese cooks are forever adding a few drops here and there. In cooking it does not so much sweeten as give an almost indefinable but undeniable piquancy to the taste.

Kitchen Utensils   There is no Japanese kitchen without both a good chopping board and very sharp knives. Cutting fish and vegetables in the Japanese way can not be done without these two essentials. Good knives are easy to come by in most countries. In Japan knives are kept sharp by storing them so they don't touch other utensils. They are often kept in a knife holder that is hung inside a kitchen cabinet. Putting a knife in a drawer with other hard objects soon leads to a knife that is only good for cutting butter.

Many Americans pick up a vegetable and start to cut it almost in the air. When I first started cooking in a Japanese kitchen I sometimes did this and it would bring peals of laughter from mother-in-law and maids alike. I would sometimes forget and peel a cucumber over the salad bowl or cut potatoes over the pot. This is a habit one quickly gets out of in Japan and it is a good habit to forget. Working on a cutting board is easier and is really the only way to get the vegetables and fish cut properly for Japanese dishes.

A good cutting or chopping board should be a block of wood two feet by ten inches. You can get a piece of unvarnished wood and treat it yourself by rubbing it with a little boiled linseed oil. Let it dry one day and it won't stain afterwards. Thick plastic boards are now available and they are sanitary for there are no cracks for food or germs to lodge in, but a good well-scrubbed chopping board is a joy to anyone who likes to cook.

A Word About Portions   A Japanese meal consists of many small dishes, and each dish contains a very small portion. This is not true for main dishes such as *nabemono;* but it is true for almost all other dishes.

Therefore, the American cook must decide if she is making a Japanese dish to be served American style or Japanese style. If American style, she may want, for instance, to give each person a whole trout. A Japanese-style portion could be much smaller, depending on how many dishes the hostess plans to serve. This is particularly true of *zensai*, because the portions will depend on how many dishes one wants to serve. In Japan, variety at a meal is the usual rule.

Portions for pickles can't be given any more accurately than portions for Western pickles can be given. Japanese eat pickles from a very tiny plate, and those who like them have seconds from the bowl of pickles on the table.

It is a point of interest here that most Japanese people are shocked at the large size of the portions served in the United States. A big meal in Japan doesn't mean large portions but many small portions from different dishes.

Chopsticks   The Japanese eat with the wooden implements which we call chopsticks and they call *hashi*. Though those used in China and elsewhere in Asia are often made of ivory (and nowadays plastic), those used in Japan are always made of wood, either plain or lacquered. They are usually brand new and joined at the top *(waribashi)* to show they have never been used. They are also fairly simple to use. Break the chopsticks apart by pulling; they will break cleanly. One of the pair is anchored firmly at the point where the thumb joins the hand and is held there by the fourth finger. The other is held by the thumb and the second and third fingers. Make certain that the tips of both sticks are even and then manipulate them with a scissorslike motion, the ball of the thumb serving as fulcrum. Food is picked up with the tips of the sticks and transferred directly to the mouth.

So much then for the explanations. With these firmly in mind we are now ready to go on to the Japanese cuisine.

Zensai—For the Beginning of the Meal

Call them hors-d'oeuvre if you will, but something definitely gets lost in the translation. It is true that *zensai* are used mostly for appetizers but there is a very different feeling to the way they are served.

Bascially, the Japanese like to party. They like to drink and it doesn't take much of an excuse for them to lift their saké, whisky or beer glasses to the toast of *kampai,* which is something like "to your health." Business dinners almost always turn out to be drinking parties and those who can hold their liquor win a lot of "face" in Japan. Actually, many Orientals don't have much tolerance for alcohol and soon get very red in the face and even get drunk, but being drunk doesn't hold the same social stigma as it does in the West, so people relax and enjoy. But in Japan, drinking calls for food and since this gets a good meal off to a grand start, that food had better look and taste good.

Zensai are small portions of cold foods. The cook aims for a variety of individual flavors from sweet to spicy. Maybe "palate teasers" would be a better way to describe them but whatever they are called, true Japanese *zensai* are prepared with the utmost care. Each tidbit turns into a conversation piece as well as a taste treat.

Like hors-d'oeuvre, they may come to the table in an artistically arranged platter. Most likely, however, they will be served in little dishes each holding just a touch of some special food. If you can picture a group of Japanese businessmen, sitting around a low table in a Japanese room drinking hot saké from tiny fragile cups and picking up bits of red caviar from tiny blue-and-white bowls, you have the true idea of Japanese appetizers.

Zensai are actually little bits and pieces of goodies served with the creative imagination that helps to express Japanese hospitality. The more formal the dinner, the more honored the guests, the more expensive and rare the little taste treats are going to be. But even in the humblest Japanese home, inexpensive soybeans can be served with care and a desire to please which makes them rightly *zensai.*

In addition, all Japanese appetizers are perfect for use in the *obento,* or Japanese lunchbox. They add bits of flavor and color to something which is otherwise mostly cold boiled rice.

Edamame (Cooked Fresh Soybeans)   In Japan, *edamame* are sold all during the summer season in their shells and still on their branches. These soybeans are called *edamame* because *eda* means branch in Japanese and *mame* means bean.

I have seen them being sold in Hawaii and in Japanese communities in California. Since the United States is one of the foremost growers of soybeans in the world, they could easily be available everywhere if everyone insisted that these delicious beans, so full of food value, be made available for people as well as cattle.

To Cook Fresh Soybeans

Take the beans off the branches and boil them in plenty of well-salted water. Don't cover the pot or beans will lose their nice green color. They should be done in 4 to 5 minutes of rapid boiling. Try one. When beans are ready, drain them and run cold water over them. Sprinkle the skins with more salt and let them cool. They seem to be a natural taste partner to a cold beer on a hot summer day.

Sweet-and-Sour Little Shrimps   These are pickled little shrimps that, served on food picks, can stand on their own as *zensai* or can be combined with other bits of food in a small bowl or on a narrow flat plate. Thinly sliced cucumbers and bits of fresh mandarin oranges with the shrimps might be just the taste and color combination that you would expect to find in an elegant Japanese restaurant. Fresh shrimps are of course considered better, but canned shrimps do very well in this pickled recipe.

Sweet-and-Sour Little Shrimps

4½ ounces canned small shrimps, or cooked shelled fresh
   shrimps
4 teaspoons sugar
4½ tablespoons vinegar
2 teaspoons *shoyu*

Rinse the shrimps under cold water to remove the oversalty taste canned shrimps can sometimes have. Mix the sugar, vinegar and *shoyu* well. Put the shrimps in the marinade in the refrigerator for about 2 hours or overnight. Drain. Put 2 or 3 shrimps on a food pick and make a pile of them on each individual plate or on a serving platter along with other foods. Makes about 12 sticks.

Black Pickled Shrimps

24 medium-size shrimps, with heads removed
Salt
3 tablespoons vinegar
1½ teaspoons sugar
1½ teaspoons salt
1 ounce fresh gingerroot
3 tablespoons *shoyu*
2 tablespoons black sesame seeds, toasted and ground

Wash and clean shrimps. Pop into salted boiling water for about 6 minutes. Drain and chill in the refrigerator. When ready to proceed, remove shells. Mix vinegar with sugar and ¾ teaspoon salt. Blend. Sprinkle the mixture over shrimps and leave to marinate in the refrigerator for 1 to 2 hours.

    Peel and mince the gingerroot and add *shoyu* and ¾ teaspoon salt. Cook this mixture over low heat, stirring constantly, until the liquid is completely reduced. Take shrimps out of the marinade, roll in the sesame seeds, and sprinkle a bit of the minced ginger on each one. Serve on food picks or on little plates.

Salmon and Raw Onion

This is basically the same dish we know in the West but it comes to the table looking a little different in Japan. The smoked salmon is sliced very thin and so are the onions. They are both put in tiny bowls for individual servings and are sometimes sprinkled with a bit of *shoyu*. For each narrow, thin slice of salmon, add a half of a slice of very thinly sliced raw onion.

Miso-Grilled Mushrooms

Fresh mushrooms are lovely served this way, but the dried *shiitake* mushrooms that are available outside of Japan do nicely too. To bring the dried mushroom back to life, soak it in cold water until soft. Pat with a paper towel. Mix 1 egg yolk and 1 tablespoon *miso*. Coat the mushrooms very well and place under the broiler or on a grill. Sprinkle with a few white sesame seeds. Can be served hot or cold. The usual Japanese serving is 2 for each person.

Pickled Japanese Mushrooms

12 dried *shiitake* mushrooms
½ cup *dashi* or stock
4 tablespoons sugar
4 tablespoons *shoyu*
1 teaspoon *mirin* (sweet saké)
1 teaspoon saké

Soak mushrooms in water for 15 minutes to soften. Remove stems. Boil caps in *dashi* for 10 to 12 minutes. Add sugar, stir, reduce heat, and continue to simmer for 15 minutes. Add *shoyu*, cook for 10 minutes, then blend in *mirin* and saké and simmer gently until the pan juices are reduced to a thick syrupy consistency. Serve cold in little dishes. The flavor and appearance of these mushrooms is a little different when sprinkled with white sesame seeds. Serves 6.

Warabi   For a fancy or unusual *zensai*, a wild or mountain vegetable may be served. A good example of this is *warabi*.

This delicacy also grows wild in the United States and other countries but no one wants to eat it. It is called bracken fern or sometimes fiddlehead or fiddler's fern. Anyone adventurous enough to have tried it knows it is best to gather it when the frond is 4 to 8 inches long. This olive-green mountain vegetable can be dried or preserved to last for over a year. This results in a loss of color but rarely a loss of flavor.

Mountain vegetables have to be treated to remove the ash taste before preparing and maybe that is why more Western people don't eat them. In Japan, they are often put in a deep bowl to which a handful of charcoal is added plus 1 tablespoon of bicarbonate of soda. Hot water is poured over this until it just covers the vegetables and then a light weight such as a plate is put on it. It is left to stand for 1 day and 1 night. Another method is to let the vegetables stand in water with 2 tablespoons of vinegar for every 2 cups of hot water. Whichever method is used, the *warabi* is boiled for 2 or 3 minutes after such treatment. It is then soaked in cold water. When it is drained it should have a bright-green appealing color.

Sauce for *Warabi*

3 tablespoons *shoyu*
3 tablespoons *mirin* or plain saké for a less sweet taste
1 tablespoon sugar

Ohitashi

Cut *warabi* about 1½ inches long and put in a deep serving bowl. Usually just a little is put into each individual bowl. Sprinkle with chopped *nori* seaweed and then pour the sauce over it. Serve chilled.

Variations

Warabi may be tossed in a green salad or served like asparagus. The sauce can be varied by adding some chopped toasted and ground peanuts or sesame seeds. Bonito shavings *(katsuobushi)* make another popular garnish for *warabi.*

Red Caviar with Grated *Daikon*

1 medium-size *daikon* radish, or substitute white turnips
1 tablespoon lemon juice
6 ounces red caviar
Lemon slices for garnish
Shoyu

Grate the *daikon* or white turnip and add the lemon juice. Gently add the red caviar without crushing the delicate eggs. Divide the mixture into 4 to 6 small bowls or dishes, and garnish with a slice of lemon. Sprinkle with just a very few drops of *shoyu*. Makes 6 small servings.

Kamaboko (Fish Cake)   *Kamaboko* is a steamed fish cake available in Oriental food stores. It comes in a small loaf and it should be refrigerated. For *zensai* just slice it fairly thin and wrap it around pieces of cucumber that have been cut into coin-sized portions and left to stand in cold water until crisp. Fasten with a food pick and put several on a small plate. For the easiest *zensai* of all, just slice the *kamaboko* into ¼-inch slices and serve on a small plate. Pour a bit of *shoyu* over both these dishes.

Little Mounds of Spinach

1 pound fresh spinach
Salt
2½ tablespoons *shoyu*
1 teaspoon sugar
1½ tablespoons white sesame seeds.

Wash the spinach. Let a very little bit of salted water come to a boil. Put the spinach in for no more than 2 minutes, drain, and run cold water over it. Drain again and sprinkle with ½ tablespoon *shoyu*. Now take the spinach by the roots and lay it out on the chopping board, squeezing any excess moisture out of it so it looks like a long piece of seaweed. Fold it over, chop off the root part and discard it. Now chop the spinach into about 1-inch-long pieces. Mix *shoyu* and sugar together and cook a minute until sugar is dissolved. Put the spinach in a bowl, pour the mixture over it, and let it stand in the refrigerator for a few hours. To serve, put each little bunch of spinach in a small bowl, pinch the top so it looks like a little mound, and garnish with the sesame seeds that have been parched in a hot dry frypan. Makes 6 small servings.

Dried Sardines Japanese

½ pound dried sardines
4 tablespoons sugar
5 tablespoons *shoyu*
2 tablespoons water

Parch dried sardines in a frypan until they are brown. They will smell very fishy while browning but this gives them better flavor. Put the sugar, *shoyu* and water in a saucepan and boil until the sugar is dissolved into a kind of syrup. Add the parched sardines and mix quickly. When the sardines are well coated, remove to a plate and let cool. Serve a few on each individual plate. Makes 4 small servings.

Ginkgo Nuts on Skewers

1 cup ginkgo nuts (about 36)
1 teaspoon salt
2 teaspoons saké

Strike the ginkgo nuts lightly to break the shells, and remove nuts from shells. The nut will have a thin inner skin. Put nuts in hot water for 5 minutes, then rub off the inner skins. Put nuts in the salt and saké and parch over heat until dry. Cool and skewer. If pine needles are available, use them as skewers, putting 2 nuts on each pine needle.

Broiled Clam Appetizers

20 to 30 clams, shelled
6 tablespoons *shoyu*
4 tablespoons *mirin*

Put 2 or 3 clams on a bamboo skewer. Continue until you have used up all the clams. Boil the *shoyu* and *mirin* until syrupy. Broil the clams lightly and baste them with the syrup.

They should be painted with the syrup about three times before being served. If you like, alternate the clams with slices of long onion or green pepper.

Quail Eggs and Chicken Balls

8 quail eggs
½ pound raw chicken, minced
Salt and pepper
1 egg, beaten
Oil for cooking
2 tablespoons water
2 teaspoons sugar
3 teaspoons *shoyu*
1 tablespoon *mirin*
1 teaspoon cornstarch

Cook eggs in boiling water for about 8 minutes, or until fully cooked. Cool under cold water and shell. Mix chicken meat with salt and pepper to taste and beaten egg to bind. Mix and shape into little balls about the same size as the quail eggs. Fry lightly in hot oil. Mix water, sugar, *shoyu* and *mirin* and bring to a boil. When sugar is dissolved, add the little chicken balls and cook over lowest possible heat for a few minutes. Dilute cornstarch with just a touch of cold water and make a smooth paste. Blend into the chicken sauce and simmer to thicken, stirring very gently. Remove from heat. Thread 1 egg and 1 chicken ball on a food pick and serve two each on a small plate to each guest.

Chicken and Mushroom Slices

3 large dried mushrooms
2 Japanese-type long onions
1 pound raw chicken, minced
1½ teaspoons *shoyu*
1½ tablespoons saké
Pinch of salt
1 teaspoon sugar
1 egg
1½ teaspoons poppy or sesame seeds

Soak mushrooms in cold water for about 10 minutes. Remove stems and dry caps on a paper towel. Mince the mushrooms and long onions and mix with the chicken; blend well. Season with *shoyu,* saké, salt and sugar, and stir in the beaten egg. Shape into a square and put in a well-greased small loaf pan. Sprinkle with the seeds and bake in a medium oven (350° F.) until cooked, about 35 minutes. Leave until cool, then remove from pan. When very cool, slice into breadlike slices and cut again into halves. Arrange 2 half slices on a plate. This recipe can also be made by shaping the meat into a square and baking it on a cookie sheet for the same amount of time. After it is cool, it can be cut into bread slices or into 12 equal squares which can be served in little individual bowls. A small dish of *shoyu* should be served along with this for dipping.

Sashimi—Raw Fish and Its Variations

The Japanese are considered either famous or infamous for eating raw fish. It depends on the gastronomical mentality of the person judging. Of course, everyone is entitled to his or her own likes and dislikes but a strong prejudice against eating *sashimi* is usually due to a lack of knowledge and experience. Westerners are often afraid to try it because they fear either an unpleasant fishy taste or smell. The Japanese, however, are very particular about their raw fish and any fish that had either would never, never be considered good enough to be served. Good Japanese *sashimi* is a great delicacy and in no way tastes strong.

Contrary to what some Westerners believe, raw fish is not an everyday food in Japan. It is a special occasion food because it is expensive. Guests are served *sashimi* in Japanese restaurants, sometimes people treat themselves to it at a *sushi* shop, and when the housewife serves it at home, it usually means there is some call for a celebration.

The most suitable fish to serve as *sashimi* are sea bream, tuna, lobster, prawns and shrimps. River fish are almost never served raw. In many restaurants in Japan, one can see tanks of fish swimming and the fish to be served is often chosen right in front of the customers' eyes. It is then prepared and brought to the tables as *sashimi* in a matter of minutes. It is not too unusual for a fish still to be wiggling, even though it has already been skillfully sliced. This can horrify some of us but it also tells one just how serious the Japanese are when it comes to serving their *sashimi* absolutely fresh.

The preparation of the fish depends a great deal on the fish itself, the occasion and the skill of the cook. Those fish that are brought to the table with head and tail intact, and only the middle sliced in the shape of scales, are done by highly professional Japanese cooks. This is very difficult to do and the technique may take years to perfect. I have known Japanese cooks skilled in this art who carry their knives back and forth from work every day for fear of something happening to these highly important tools of their trade. The knives are kept razor sharp, are of the best quality steel, and are often wrapped with loving care in paper, then covered with cloth. When you understand this, you will know that this book is not going to try to teach you this art.

But such a fancy presentation is not a must and the fish can be cut into slices and cubes and still be served in a most artistic way. Creative thought goes into the color of the fish meat, the color of the dish and the garnish.

To prepare *sashimi:* scale 1 very fresh fish. Remove head, tail and fins. Clean out and discard viscera. Wash fish thoroughly and leave to soak in cold water for a few minutes. Adding a bit of ice to this water helps make the flesh firm. Remove all bones and skin and cut flesh into fillets. You will need a very sharp knife and a good cutting board. Cut the fillets at an angle into slices. Firm-fleshed fish can be cut into 1- or ½-inch slices or can be sliced about 1 to 1½ inches wide and about ¼ inch thick. Thin-fleshed fish is cut into thin slivers. The cutting is always slanted and always uniform.

If the *sashimi* planned is prawns, lobster or the like, they must be kept alive until you are ready to prepare them. Kill shellfish quickly by stabbing them with a knife in the soft part of the belly. Shell them and wash the flesh. Soak in ice water and the flesh will soon become firm.

The *sashimi* can be arranged on 1 large plate or served in small individual plates. In Japan, these individual plates are often long and narrow. Along with this a small dish of *shoyu* is served. The serving dish is decorated with various garnishes that are also dipped into the *shoyu* and eaten along with the fish. Grated horseradish, *wasabi,* is served as a very important part of the garnish and a pinch of it is mixed into each personal little plate of *shoyu.* This is the dipping sauce.

Thin-sliced raw vegetables also make up the garnish and it is up to the cook to create them. In Japan a vegetable called *udo* is usually served with *sashimi* but shredded celery can be a good substitute when *udo* is not available. Lettuce,

44

watercress and parsley can also be used to make up the edible garnish for *sashimi*. If fresh *wasabi* is not available, instant *wasabi* can be found in almost all stores carrying Oriental foods. It comes in a powdered form and a few drops of water makes a paste that has a flavor very like fresh horseradish. The combination of a bit of hot *wasabi* and *shoyu* to mix and dip your *sashimi* into gives a flavor that is truly Japanese.

Suggestions for *Sashimi*

Sea Bream *Sashimi*

Prepare as described. As this is a delicate-fleshed fish, cut the slices very thin, about ½ inch thick. Garnish with watercress, parsley and horseradish that is piled into a cone-shaped heap.

Shrimp *Sashimi*

Prepare and shell as described, cutting off the heads. Place in ice water and pat dry with a paper towel. Arrange on a bed of thinly sliced lettuce or thinly sliced cabbage. Add grated horseradish and 2 teaspoons of fresh grated gingerroot.

Lobster *Sashimi* in Its Own Shell

Prepare as described above, taking the flesh out of the shell but keeping the shell intact. Put the flesh in ice water. Boil the shell for a few minutes until it turns red; chill the shell. Cut the lobster into bite-sized chunks or tear into pieces by hand. Turn the shell with open side uppermost and line it with shredded lettuce, shredded *daikon* radish or any garnish that makes a nice bed for the meat. Place the meat back in the shell and serve with mounds of grated horseradish. Provide a small plate for each person for the *shoyu*.

There are of course many more possibilities to the art of serving raw fish Japanese style. These are just a few. Actually most Japanese housewives today go down to the local fish market and have the fishmonger cut the fish a little while before dinner time. Anyone wanting to try this Japanese fish adventure outside of Japan, however, now has enough information to do it with style.

Yakimono—Broiled Foods

In Japanese *yaki* can mean "burn" while *mono* simply means "thing." When it comes to food, however, *yakimono* doesn't mean burned food but foods that have been grilled or broiled to the point of making them browned or crisp on the outside and tender in the middle. It is a form of Japanese cooking that everyone seems to love, and it is perfect for the outdoor-cooking fan as well as for those who watch their waistlines. All kinds of foods can be cooked this way, and there is a lot of room for playing with the sauces and food combinations to suit your own tastes and caloric needs.

Probably the most popular of Japanese *yakimono* is *yakitori,* that is, chicken grilled on skewers and brushed with a sauce. Usually this sauce is made of *dashi,* saké and *shoyu* and it is brushed on before and during the cooking. Sometimes the sauce is omitted and the foods are grilled with only salt and this is called *shioyaki.*

Yakitori shops are found all over Japan and if they are even half good, they are sure to be successful—a favorite place for office workers to go after work. By six in the evening, most city *yakitori* shops are packed with people enjoying their chicken with cold beer or hot saké. As one passes one of these shops in the evening, the delicious smell teases the nose and invites the passerby in. Since they are mostly informal, rather reasonably priced counter-shops, it is easy to give into the temptation. Most *yakitori* shops serve a variety of vegetables grilled along with this chicken Japanese style.

Besides the *shioyaki* style, another way of flavoring the foods before broiling is by putting the fish or meat into *miso* for two or three days before cooking it. *Miso* gives the foods a very individual taste and one that most Japanese peo-

ple are very fond of. Often, vinegar-flavored or sweet boiled
vegetables are served along with *miso*-flavored *yakimono.*

Chicken Breast *Yakitori* Style

½ pound boneless breast of chicken, diced into small bite-
   size pieces

Sauce
   3 tablespoons *shoyu*
   4 tablespoons saké
   2 tablespoons sugar
   1 tablespoon *mirin*

Put all the ingredients for the sauce into a pan and bring to a
gentle boil. When the liquid is reduced to half, remove from
the heat and cool. Increase the recipe by several times if you
have lots of grilling to do. This same sauce is good for all *yakitori* recipes, including the variations of this dish.

   After the pieces of chicken have been washed and dried
with a paper towel, thread them carefully on bamboo skewers. This can also be done in advance if the chicken is refrigerated while it is waiting to be grilled.

   Dip each of the skewers into the sauce and grill until
brown, turning so chicken pieces will brown on all sides, and
basting with the sauce from time to time. Serve several skewers to each person on a small plate and have hot pepper available to sprinkle on the chicken. Makes 4 small servings.

Yakitori **Variations**   In Japan, *yakitori* is not just made with
choice pieces of chicken breast. It is also made with chicken
livers, diced giblets or even chicken skin. Diced vegetables
are also put on the skewers along with the meat, or separately
on their own skewers but cut and cooked in the same way, to
be served with the *yakitori*. Alternate pieces of leeks and
chicken make up a very popular combination for *yakimono.*

   There are many other foods you can put on the skewers and make in this way. Bite-size pieces of onion, green
pepper, small eggplants, mushrooms, lotus roots and peeled
slices of sweet potato. Like so many other Japanese dishes,
the basic rules are there but the variety and combinations are

all up to the individual cook. For *yakitori,* a sauce is often made and served alongside in another small dish for dipping. This is optional but very good and adds a lot. It is made by grating *daikon,* that large Japanese radish. To a small pile of grated *daikon,* a pinch of grated fresh gingerroot and a pinch of freshly ground pepper add a lot of taste.

Some people like to break a quail egg in the middle of this and pour a bit of *shoyu* over it. It is mixed with chopsticks and is a perfect dipping sauce. If *daikon* is not available, you might try grating a turnip and using about 1 teaspoon ground ginger in it.

Grilled Trout

Dress the trout, remove the viscera, but leave the head and tail intact.

Sauce—enough for 2 medium-size or 4 small fish
½ cup *shoyu*
½ cup saké
2 tablespoons sugar
or
½ cup *shoyu*
½ cup saké
1 long onion, chopped very fine

Mix the ingredients of whichever sauce appeals to you. Let the fish stand in the mixture for 30 minutes, turning it over from time to time. Place on a hot grill in your broiler, basting with the sauce about three times. Grill slowly and carefully until golden brown on each side. Serve hot with lemon. Makes 4 small servings.

Grilled Fillets of Fish

4 fillets of white fish, or about 1 pound filleted rockfish or
    mackerel

Make whichever of the sauces you want and cook fish fillets in the same way as the grilled trout. Squeeze lemon juice over fillets and serve hot, perhaps with a bit of ginger. Makes 4 small servings.

Shioyaki (Salt-Grilled Fish)

Sprinkle fish or fish fillets with ½ teaspoon salt for every pound of fish and let stand for at least 30 minutes. If you are using a whole fish, make sure it is well cleaned but that the tail and head are intact. Just before grilling sprinkle another teaspoon of salt on the fish or fillets and broil or grill. Squeeze lemon juice over fillets and serve hot. A bit of fresh gingerroot is very good along with this.

Miso-Grilled Fish

This can be done with most fish but haddock is suggested.

3 fillets of haddock
Salt
1½ pounds white *miso* paste
4 tablespoons saké
2 tablespoons sugar

Cut the fillets into halves to make 6 portions. Sprinkle with a very little salt and let stand while you are preparing the *miso* mixture. Mix *miso,* saké and sugar. Spread half this mixture in a deep pan, lay a piece of muslin cloth over it, put the fillets on top, cover with the muslin, and spread with the remaining *miso.* Put fish in the refrigerator for 2 to 3 days. Just before grilling, unwrap and wipe very lightly with a paper towel. This way fillets can be kept longer; it is a convenient way to preserve fish. Makes 6 small servings.

Miso-Grilled Meat

3 pork cutlets
1½ pounds dark *miso*
4 tablespoons saké
3 tablespoons sugar

Cut each cutlet into halves to make 6 portions. Mix *miso,* saké and sugar. Spread half this mixture in a deep pan, lay a piece of muslin cloth over it, put the meat on top, cover with the muslin, and spread with the remaining *miso.* Put in the refrigerator until ready to cook. Just before grilling, unwrap, but wipe very lightly with a paper towel. Makes 6 small servings.

Grilled Lobsters Japanese

3 medium-size lobsters
1½ tablespoons salt
5 tablespoons *shoyu*
2 tablespoons *mirin*
1 teaspoon powdered Japanese pepper, or 2 teaspoons red
    pepper

Broil the lobsters in salt water for about 15 minutes. Cool,
and remove the feelers and legs. If they are American lobsters, make slashes in the large claws. Cut the lobsters half
through and put in a mixture of *shoyu* and *mirin.* Turn several
times to coat well. Broil over hot coals, brushing the lobsters
with this mixture. Serve with red pepper. A good combination with this dish is chilled pickled lotus root. Makes 3
servings.

Glazed and Grilled Squid   Squid is enjoyed in Japan and
the Japanese have many ways of preparing it, including eating it raw. Dried and seasoned squid is sold wherever people
go, from train stations to the baseball park, and wherever
they might want something to chew on. It is considered
tasty eaten along with alcoholic drinks and the slightly salty
squid can indeed taste very good with cold beer. Squid is a
very common food in Japan and the Japanese cook feels as
much at home with a fresh squid as the Western cook feels
with a beef steak.

Glazed Squid

12 small squids
3 tablespoons saké
1 teaspoon salt
2½ teaspoons sugar

Wash squid in several waters. With great care empty the ink
bags but keep the "ink." Make a few very shallow "scratch"
incisions on each squid. Combine saké, salt and sugar, bring
to a boil, add "ink," stir well and as soon as it boils again
add all the squids. Reduce heat and simmer very gently until
they are tender, taking them out with a perforated spoon.

Reduce liquid until it is quite thick. Brush squid with liquid and put under the broiler or on hot grill. Broil for a few minutes until nicely crisp and brown. Serve with a bit of grated *daikon* radish. Grated turnip can be used in place of *daikon*.

Grilled Salted Shrimps

12 large shrimps, peeled
Salt
1½ teaspoons black sesame seeds
Juice of 1 lemon
Shoyu, equivalent to lemon juice

Cut shrimps lengthwise, slitting them without cutting through completely. Remove vein, flatten shrimp gently, sprinkle with salt and sesame seeds. Grill seasoned side first, then turn and grill the other side. Arrange 2 shrimps in each individual serving dish. Mix lemon juice with equal amount of *shoyu* and serve as an accompanying sauce. The shrimps are dipped into this mixture.

Miso-Grilled Vegetables

Vegetables—whatever you fancy: green beans, lima beans, cauliflowerets, sliced carrots, etc.
Miso paste
Egg yolks

Cook the vegetables a bit, but not until they are soft. They should be semicooked. Then make a mixture of 1 tablespoon *miso* to every egg yolk needed to make enough marinade for the amount of vegetables you will be cooking. Let these partly cooked vegetables sit in the sauce for a time—usually up to half an hour—turning them to coat them well. Then broil or grill the *miso*-covered vegetables and serve hot.

Peanut-Grilled Carrots

Of course grilling with peanuts is not a traditional Japanese method but I was served this at a Japanese home and the cook told me she got the recipe from a modern Japanese women's magazine. I have used it ever since and thought you might enjoy this recipe—something Japanese cooks make right now.

1 pound carrots, scraped
10 peanuts, shelled
4 tablespoons *dashi* or stock
1½ tablespoons sugar
2 tablespoons saké
2 raw egg yolks

Wash the carrots and cut into attractive uniform pieces. Little chunks are fine as they will hold on a skewer. Put them on a bamboo skewer. Pound peanuts in a mortar into a smooth paste and put into a bowl. Gradually add *dashi* or stock, sugar and saké. Stir egg yolks and blend into the mixture. Dip the skewered carrots into this mixture, grill and serve. Other firm vegetables can be served this way and it is especially good with slices of sweet potato.

Unagi no Kabayaki (Grilled Eel)

4 small eels
Salt
1 cup *shoyu*
1 tablespoon *mirin*
1 tablespoon saké
3 tablespoons sugar

Split the eels down the back, remove bones, and cut into ½-inch lengths. Sprinkle with salt. Mix *shoyu, mirin,* saké and sugar and boil the mixture for several minutes until the sugar is dissolved. Thread the eel pieces on skewers, dip into the sauce, and cook on a hot grill for 8 to 10 minutes, brushing frequently with the sauce. Turn as you cook and make sure both sides are nicely browned. Makes 6 to 8 small servings.

Sazae no Tsuboyaki (Grilled Turbo Cooked in the Shell)

This recipe calls up many a fond memory of the beaches along the Japan Sea. Whenever you are with a group of Japanese people there is generally no shortage of excellent swimmers and these shells were a favorite for the young people to dive for. Often our group would soon have a pile of turbo shells and the most natural thing in the world to do was to make a fire and cook them. On the beach we roasted them without chestnuts or spinach but this is a fancier version.

4 turbos
4 ounces spinach
Salt
4 dried mushrooms
⅔ cup *dashi* or stock
6 chestnuts (canned will do)
5 tablespoons *shoyu*
Pinch of sugar
1 tablespoon saké

Boil the turbos in their shells or roast on an open fire. Allow to cool, take out the flesh, and slice, removing only the end. The Japanese also use the green part but you may want to discard this. Wash spinach, dust with salt, and cook in a little boiling water for only 1 minute. Drain and cut up. Soak mushrooms in water to soften; remove stems. Cook caps in a few tablespoons of *dashi* or stock for a few minutes; drain and slice. Mash the chestnuts and mix with the turbo meat. Add the spinach, mashed chestnuts and sliced mushrooms. Season with a mixture of 2 tablespoons *dashi*, 1 teaspoon *shoyu* and a pinch of sugar. Blend well and fill shells with the mixture. Mix remainder of the *dashi* and *shoyu* and saké, spoon a little of this liquid mixture into each shell to seal it, and put back on the grill to heat through. Serve hot in the shell. Makes 4 servings.

Nimono—Boiled Foods

There is no doubt about it, a Japanese cook would be absolutely lost without a big bottle of *shoyu*. In Japan, it flavors just about all foods and very good flavoring it is too, but one can't help wondering how this all got started.

It came from China in ancient times and it must have been a great boon to all those pots of bland foods cooked over open fires in Japan. Like all other imports to Japan, the Japanese soon changed it to suit their taste and the *shoyu* became a lighter seasoning than soy sauce from China. It is still very much used to flavor boiled foods, and this Japanese way of cooking is called *nimono*.

Nimono consists of many kinds of foods boiled and flavored with a sauce of, basically, *shoyu,* saké, *dashi* or, sometimes, *miso.* The foods that go into the pot with this sauce can be fish, meat, shellfish, vegetables or bean curds. Although there are certainly favorite combinations, the cook is free to make up a *nimono* of whatever is desired or, more likely, available.

This way of serving plain foods boiled with a basic sauce is a very old Japanese form of cooking and it saved me many times when I first came to Japan. Living in the country and not being able to read Japanese, I often had the experience of coming back from the local store with a can of something that was totally different from what I imagined from the picture on the can. I recall one time in particular opening a mystery can that turned out to be scallops. I was preparing dinner with my Japanese mother-in-law and was too proud to confess that I didn't know what I had bought. There was a pot with a leftover *nimono* of carrots and turnips in the refrigerator so I broke up the scallops, dumped the whole thing, juice and all, into the leftovers, heated it up, and added a few snow peas just before serving it. My mother-in-law thought it genius to change the flavor and thus use last night's *nimono*. To my amusement, it became an Itoh family favorite recipe.

I would call *nimono* "down-home" Japanese cooking. It can be dressed up and served in fancy Japanese restaurants, since no real Japanese meal is complete without it, but it is a favorite in farmhouses and tiny city flats as well.

Many Japanese housewifes find *nimono* a very practical way to cook. It is almost always cooked in advance. Served hot or cold it is sure to please. Yesterday's *nimono* often finds its way into the lunchboxes of today in the form of pieces of flavored fish, meat and vegetables to go along with the rice. It is a natural partner for rice and it is very much a part of the elaborate "before" cooking that takes place just before the three-day New Year's holiday. One of the graces of the *nimono* is that the flavors don't suffer when it is cooked again and reheated.

Vegetables and Minced Chicken *Nimono*

1 large turnip and 1 eggplant, or 2 cucumbers or potatoes
4 cups chicken soup
1½ teaspoons salt
8 ounces raw chicken, minced
3 tablespoons *mirin*
3 tablespoons *shoyu*
2 teaspoons cornstarch

Peel the turnip or other vegetables and cut into 5 cubes about 1½ inches square; cut each cube into slices vertically, but don't cut quite through to the base. Then cut these slices similarly at a right angle and you will find they form something like little fan shapes. Add 4 cups of chicken soup and the salt. Boil gently until vegetables are tender.

Remove vegetables and add ½ cup of the liquid in which vegetables were cooked to the minced chicken, *mirin* and *shoyu*. Bring to a boil and cook until chicken is tender. Mix 2 teaspoons of water with the cornstarch, add to the boiling mixture, and cook until the liquid thickens. Put some of the vegetables in a small bowl for each person. Pour the thick sauce with the minced chicken over it. Makes 4 servings.

Fish *Miso Nimono*

1 pound fish
1 cup water
2 tablespoons saké
3 tablespoons sugar
5 tablespoons *miso*
1 ounce gingerroot, grated

Cut the fish lengthwise into 2 pieces. Then cut the upper and lower slices into 3, making 6 pieces. Mackerel is usually used for this dish. Put the water, saké, sugar and *miso* in a saucepan and boil. When this boils, put in the pieces of fish, skin side up, and boil over medium heat for about 10 minutes.

Put 1 piece of fish on each medium-size dish and pour over the liquid in which it was boiled. Put grated ginger on top and serve. Makes 4 servings.

Daikon with Chicken Sauce

Cook 1 medium-size *daikon* radish (turnip can be used in place of *daikon*), diced or cubed, in 4 cups of *dashi,* with 1 tablespoon sugar and 2 tablespoons *shoyu* added, until tender.

When cooked tender, remove with a slotted spoon and set aside. Take 1½ cups of the stock the *daikon* was cooked in and add about 7 ounces ground raw chicken. Add 1 teaspoon sugar, 2 tablespoons *shoyu* and 1 tablespoon saké and cook until sauce begins to thicken. Mix and pour over the *daikon.*

This recipe can be made with eggplant too.

Pork and Ginger *Nimono*

2 pounds white turnips
4 Japanese long onions
1 ounce fresh gingerroot, minced, or 1 tablespoon ground
    ginger
4 cups water
1½ tablespoons saké
1 pound pork, cut into bite-size pieces
3 tablespoons *shoyu*
2 tablespoons sugar

Peel the turnips (you can use potatoes if you like) and dice. Mince the onions very fine and mix with minced gingerroot or ground ginger.

Bring the water to a boil and add the saké, long onions and ginger. Add pork and turnip, reduce heat, and simmer gently for 1 hour. Add *shoyu* and sugar, simmering for another 5 to 7 minutes. Serve in individual bowls. Makes 6 to 8 small servings.

Pumpkin or Squash with Ground Beef *Nimono*

1 pound pumpkin or squash, approximately
2 pieces fresh gingerroot
½ pound ground beef
¾ cup basic *dashi* or beef stock
1 tablespoon cornstarch
1 tablespoon cold water

Sauce
2 tablespoons saké
2 tablespoons sugar
3 tablespoons *shoyu*

Cut squash or pumpkin into uniform pieces about 1½ inches long. With spoon, scrape out seeds and any stringy parts. Round the edges for a prettier look. Cut half the gingerroot into thin strips; soak in water to make crisp. Chop the remaining gingerroot.

In a pan place chopped ginger and the well-mixed sauce ingredients. Heat, add the ground beef, and stir constantly until the liquid is almost gone. Place squash or pumpkin in a pan, add the *dashi* or stock, and cover. Bring to a boil. Reduce heat and simmer until tender. Remove squash or pumpkin to a plate and bring the remaining mixture to a boil, stirring in 1 tablespoon of cornstarch dissolved in 1 tablespoon cold water. Add this to the ground beef mixture and simmer 2 minutes. Spoon the meat mixture over the squash and garnish with the gingerroot strips. Makes 4 servings.

Boiled Green Beans and Eggs

12 ounces green snap beans
½ cup basic *dashi* or chicken stock
2 tablespoons *shoyu*
2 tablespoons sugar
2 eggs

Prepare the beans by stringing if necessary and snapping off the ends. Cut each bean into halves and boil with *dashi* or stock, *shoyu* and sugar. When soft, beat the eggs and pour over them; cover, and steam until eggs are firm.

     This can be spooned out onto a serving plate or platter or can be cut into fourths and served on small individual plates. Makes 4 servings.

Bamboo, Mushroom and Snow Peas *Nimono*

1 pound bamboo shoots, sliced into julienne strips or cut
   into rounds
4 tablespoons *shoyu*
4 tablespoons water
2½ tablespoons *mirin*
10 dried *shiitake* mushrooms
¼ pound snow peas
2 tablespoons white sesame seeds

Cook bamboo shoots in a mixture of *shoyu,* water and *mirin* until tender. Soak the mushrooms for about 10 minutes. Remove stems and slice caps. When bamboo shoots are cooked, remove with a slotted spoon and cook the mushrooms in the same sauce for about 5 minutes. One minute before turning off the heat, add the snow peas. Then turn off the heat. Put the mushrooms, snow peas and what is left of the liquid over the bamboo shoots in a bowl. Serve in 6 individual bowls and sprinkle each with white sesame seeds. This is served either hot or cold.

Stuffed Cabbage Rolls Japanese

6 large cabbage leaves
½ pound boneless pork, minced
4 Japanese leeks, finely chopped
2 teaspoons salt
2 teaspoons sugar
1 tablespoon saké
1 egg, beaten
2 cups *dashi*
3 tablespoons *shoyu*
1 lotus root, about 3 inches long
Snow peas for garnish

Wash cabbage leaves, trim off thick edges, drop into a pan of boiling water for 30 seconds, just enough to make leaves tender, and drain. Mix pork with leeks and season with 1 teaspoon salt and 1 teaspoon sugar. Add saké and egg and stir well. Stuff each cabbage leaf by laying it flat, spreading the meat over it, and rolling it up; tie it with thread to prevent unrolling. Bring *dashi* to a boil, add *shoyu* and remaining salt and sugar. Put in cabbage rolls and simmer gently until they are thoroughly permeated with flavor. Slice the lotus root and add it to the dish about 10 minutes before it is done. Add the snow peas 3 or 4 minutes before turning off the heat. Take cabbage rolls out carefully with a perforated spoon, remove threads, cut each roll into 1-inch lengths, and serve with lotus and snow peas, and with the sauce poured over it all. Makes 6 servings.

Boiled Turnips Japanese Style

1 pound young turnips
2 cups water
4 tablespoons sugar
2 pieces of *kuruma-fu* (see page 29)
1½ teaspoons salt
2 tablespoons *shoyu*

Scrub the turnips and dry. Scrape off any blemished parts but it is all right to leave the skins on. Slice or dice. Bring the water to a boil with the sugar, and cook the turnips in this liquid for 20 minutes. Soak *fu* in water for about 5 minutes. Shred and add to turnips. Add salt and *shoyu* to taste, and continue to cook for about 10 minutes, or until the turnips are tender. Makes 6 servings.

Boiled Shrimps and Cauliflower

12 shrimps
4 tablespoons *shoyu*
4 tablespoons water
2½ tablespoons *mirin*
1 small cauliflower
6 ounces shelled peas

Clean shrimps, remove heads, and boil in a mixture of *shoyu,* water and *mirin.* When ready, take the shrimps out with a perforated spoon and keep hot. Cook the cauliflower, divided into small flowerets, in the liquid left over from the shrimps. Add peas and cook just until tender. Serve shrimps, cauliflower and peas together in small bowls, allowing 2 shrimps per portion. Makes 6 servings.

Mackerel *Nimono*

6 tablespoons *shoyu*
4 tablespoons *mirin*
4 tablespoons saké
1½ tablespoons sugar
4 mackerel fillets
4 slices of lime or lemon

Mix *shoyu, mirin,* saké and sugar, bring to a boil, and add the mackerel. Cover and simmer over very low heat for 30 minutes. Serve in individual dishes with the sauce poured over the fish, and garnish with lemon or lime slices. Makes 4 servings.

Mushimono—Steamed Foods

Those who are seriously concerned with good nutrition will probably agree that steaming is a good way to prepare food. This oil-free method doesn't boil away precious food values and it is easy on the digestive system. Maybe it is too good because it has always had a slightly negative connotation to it. Steamed foods used to remind me of cooking for someone who was not well. That attitude completely changed after living in Japan.

There is nothing dull or uninteresting about this traditional Japanese cooking method. The foods are usually steamed in decorative individual bowls or cups and served as they come from the steaming kettle. Sometimes the food is steamed in one pan but still dished out carefully to be served in small portions in individual bowls. One steamed dish is often called for in a traditional Japanese meal and that helps to give the meal great variety.

Probably the best-known of Japanese steamed dishes is *chawan-mushi* which is best described as a nondessert custard. This was a surprise to me at first because custards were always sweet where I came from. *Chawan-mushi* is an egg custard, but it is a custard steamed in a special cup and it contains whatever the cook fancies. This makes it fun to create as you can add pieces of chicken, fish, vegetables and mushrooms. It is a delight to have a good *chawan-mushi* prepared by a creative cook as it is always a surprise to see how many little bits of taste treasures can be hidden in the cup of hot custard.

Oriental steaming pots are available in some Oriental stores but no need to fret if you don't have one. Instead take a good, large sturdy pot and put in enough water to come 1½ inches up the sides. Set a heatproof bowl upside down in the pot and place a plate with the food to be steamed on top. You can set the little cups with food in them on this plate too. Just bring the water to a boil, cover the pot tightly, and steam the food gently.

Chawan-Mushi

4 ounces raw chicken, sliced
Shoyu
2 ounces dried mushrooms
12 ginkgo nuts
4 cups basic *dashi* or chicken stock
Salt
4 eggs
½ *kamaboko* portion
2 ounces spinach
8 raw shrimps, peeled
2 thin slices of lemon

Sprinkle chicken with 1 teaspoon *shoyu* and leave to stand for 15 minutes. Soak mushrooms in cold water to soften; trim off stems. Shell ginkgo nuts and boil to remove outer layer of flesh. Heat *dashi* or stock, season to taste with salt and *shoyu,* and leave to cool. Beat eggs, whisk into cold *dashi,* and strain. Cut *kamaboko* diagonally into neat slices. Dip cleaned spinach into hot water for a second; trim ends to a uniform length. Divide all ingredients, including shrimps, equally into 4 portions. Decorate with little bunches of spinach and fill with egg and *dashi* mixture. Cover the bowls, put in a steamer, and steam gently until set, about 15 minutes. Put ½ slice of lemon on the top. Serve custard in the same bowl it was cooked in. Makes 4 servings.

Steamed Vegetables with *Miso* Sauce   Steamed foods can be very bland and seasoning is desirable. A nutritious and tasty sauce made of *miso* is a perfect combination with vegetables that have been steamed.

Miso Sauce

2 tablespoons each of white and red *miso* paste
1 cup saké
1 tablespoon sugar
1 egg yolk

Mix and cook over low heat until completely hot and sticky. Pour over any steamed food. Very good over eggplant, pumpkin, squash or steamed cucumbers. A garnish of white sesame seeds adds to the flavor. Makes enough sauce for 4 servings.

Stuffed Pumpkin Japanese

1 small pumpkin, about 2 pounds
Salt
1 block of *tofu*, about 10 ounces
3 dried mushrooms
2 teaspoons sugar
1 carrot, diced
8 ounces raw chicken, minced
1 cup chicken stock
1 teaspoon cornstarch
1 tablespoon cold water

Cut top of pumpkin off and keep for use as a lid. The pumpkin serves both as the main vegetable and as the cooking pot for this dish. Remove seeds and sprinkle inside of the pumpkin with salt. Squeeze surplus moisture out of the *tofu* in a muslin bag. Soak mushrooms in water to soften, remove stems, and cut caps into strips. Mash the *tofu* thoroughly to eliminate all lumps, add ½ teaspoon salt, the sugar, carrot, mushrooms and chicken. Mix well; stuff pumpkin with mixture and steam until tender. Steam the lid separately. Flavor stock with salt and heat. Dilute cornstarch with water and blend into hot stock. Cook until sauce thickens, stirring constantly. Cover pumpkin with its lid, pour sauce over the whole and serve. Chopped prawns and peas may be substituted for chicken and carrots. Makes 4 servings.

Cold Steamed Chicken

If you enjoy cooking, you probably have hundreds of chicken recipes already and will be glad to have another one. The Japanese way of making steamed chicken is tasty and, since it is served cold, it is an ideal dish for a hot summer evening that can be prepared in the cool of the morning.

½ pound raw breast of chicken
2 tablespoons saké
2 tablespoons *shoyu*
2 tablespoons vinegar
1 teaspoon sugar
½ teaspoon dry mustard
Salt

Skin chicken. Combine the saké and *shoyu* and sprinkle it over the meat, rubbing it in with your hands. Steam chicken until tender. Remove, chill, shred into small pieces. Mix vinegar, sugar and mustard and salt to taste. Dip the small pieces of chicken in the dressing and serve. Not traditional, but good served on a bed of shredded lettuce. Makes 2 to 4 small servings.

Mushrooms Steamed in Little Earthen Pots

This is a very elegant dish to the Japanese as *matsutake* or pine mushrooms are usually used in this recipe. Pine mushrooms are very expensive and only available for a short time during the autumn but they are considered the peak of culinary pleasures in Japan. In some places in the U.S.A. pine tree mushrooms may occasionally be available, but this recipe is also very good made with any other type of mushroom. The pots for this dish are available in Japan in any pottery shop. They look like little teapots but teacups with covers will do almost as well.

6 large or 12 small mushrooms
2 tablespoons saké
1 teaspoon salt
6 ounces raw chicken or white-fleshed fish
12 small pieces of watercress
24 ginkgo nuts, or 12 small chestnuts
1½ cups *dashi* or chicken stock
½ teaspoon salt
1 teaspoon *shoyu*
1 tablespoon bitter orange juice or lemon juice

Remove the stems of the mushrooms, wash caps, cut lengthwise into 4 pieces, and put in the mixture of saké and salt. Slice the chicken or fish into small bite-size pieces; sprinkle with the saké in which the mushrooms were soaking. Cut the watercress into 1-inch-long pieces.

Parch the ginkgo nuts a little, remove the shells, put them into hot water, and peel off the thin skins. If chestnuts are used, remove the shells and skins the same way. Put raw mushrooms, chicken, nuts and watercress into 6 earthen pots, add the mixture of stock, salt and *shoyu* and put them over heat or, if teacups with covers are used, put the covered teacups into water and steam gently for about 15 minutes. If the earthen teapots are used, plug up the spouts with the skin of a lemon. Serve hot and have each guest pour the soup into the cup lids and add the orange or lemon juice. Dip the ingredients into this and eat. If the teacups are used, spoon out some of the soup into a saké cup and dip the foods into that. Makes 6 servings.

Fish and *Tofu* Steamed in Saké

4 spinach leaves
4 fillets of white fish
1 block of *tofu,* about 10 ounces
¼ cup saké
Dash of *shoyu*
4 pieces of *nori* seaweed
1 lemon

Remove any tough stems and ribs from spinach. Blanch the leaves by pouring very hot water over them. Drain, run cold water over them, put in a paper towel, and set aside. Cut the fillets into 2 pieces each and cube the *tofu* into 8 pieces. Put fish and *tofu* in a bowl, pour the saké over it, add a dash of *shoyu,* and set the bowl in a steaming pan.

Add the spinach leaves and the *nori* seaweed that has been cut into strips. Place this on top like a garnish, cover, and steam for about 40 minutes. Serve sprinkled with lemon juice. The finished dish can be served into little bowls, or it can be steamed in 4 separate little bowls. Makes 4 servings.

Steamed Trout

4 small or 2 medium-size trout
1 teaspoon salt

Dipping Sauce

For each person:

1 tablespoon *shoyu*

1 tablespoon lemon juice

2 tablespoons *dashi* or stock

1 tablespoon thinly sliced long onion

2 tablespoons grated *daikon* radish

Scale the fish, removing all the viscera. Wipe with a paper towel and make a deep cut in the middle of each fish. This should be centered between the head and tail but do not cut through the fish. Sprinkle with the salt. Steam from 10 to 20 minutes, depending on the size of the fish, until the flesh breaks easily with a fork.

Make the dipping sauce, mixing the above ingredients for each person. Serve in individual bowls. Serve the fish on a separate plate and let each person dip the fish in the little bowl of sauce. Makes 4 servings.

Sunomono and *Aemono*—
Japanese Dressed Foods

Sunomono   You might find it thrilling to make a dish that was prepared over a thousand years ago. One of the oldest written recipes in Japan is still eaten and enjoyed today. The dish is called *sunomono* and it was mentioned in the *Nihon Shoki,* one of the oldest histories of Japan.

Every Japanese knows about the *Nihon Shoki.* It is a kind of Japanese bible telling many, many things about ancient Japan, including how the Emperor's ancestors were believed to have come from heaven and how they settled in the islands that are now Japan. Since the end of World War II, most Japanese no longer take everything written in this book literally, but *sunomono* was actually mentioned in that text and it is still a very important part of Japanese cuisine.

In the Japanese language, *su* means "vinegar" and *no* comes close to showing possession. *Mono* just means "thing," so perhaps the closest translation we can get is: vinegared food. We certainly don't want to call it just vinegared thing— that would leave too much to the imagination and we are really talking about a very definite Japanese dish.

Sunomono is the original Japanese version of salad. It has a delightful, sour, yet slightly sweet flavor. This has a cleansing effect on the palate, which prepares one for the next Japanese taste treat on the menu. Low in calories and good in taste, *sunomono* is ideal for a side dish served with the main luncheon or dinner fare.

There are many kinds of ingredients that can be made into *sunomono*. Fish and octopus, exotic things like edible chrysanthemum flowers and the large radishlike *daikon*. Using the basic *sunomono* sauce, you can turn cucumbers, crab and many other foods that are common all over the world into truly classic Japanese cuisine.

When trying *sunomono* it might be wise to start with the simple cucumber *sunomono*. All one needs is cucumbers and the makings for the sauce. This may take a little experimenting because the basic sauce is a matter of taste. Some like it half vinegar and half *shoyu* with no sugar. Some add a bit of salt to that. Others like equal parts of vinegar, *shoyu* and *mirin*. Then again there are others who like twice as much vinegar as sugar, with a touch of salt. Below is my favorite version of the basic sauce and it suits my Western taste very well. I might add that the Japanese who ate my *sunomono* seemed to like it too.

Basic *Sunomono* Sauce

2 tablespoons vinegar
1 tablespoon sugar
1 tablespoon *mirin*
½ teaspoon salt
2 teaspoons *shoyu*

Cucumber *Sunomono*

2 cucumbers

The smaller and younger cucumbers will make a better *sunomono*. Cut them into thin circular slices. Although it is not a traditional Japanese method, I use a potato peeler to get them as thin as an expert Japanese cook does. Mix the ingredients for the sauce, pour it over the cucumbers, and let the mixture stand in the refrigerator for an hour or so. Serve in individual small bowls.

For a slight variation of this, try adding small parts of either a mandarin or navel orange. Peel the orange and remove all membrane and skin. If it is a large orange, cut sections into 3 pieces. Canned mandarin oranges are nice for this recipe. This mixture has a delightful flavor and the color combination looks refreshing. Follow the basic recipe, mixing the oranges with the cucumbers.

Other combinations with crab or shrimps are excellent. The following are some more good suggestions.

Crab and Cucumber *Sunomono*

2 cucumbers
6½ ounces crab meat, drained
Basic *sunomono* sauce (see page 70)
Grated lemon rind

Prepare cucumber as in cucumber *sunomono*. Mix cucumber and crab together, being careful to remove all the paperlike cartilage from the crab meat. Mix sauce and marinate the crab and cucumber for about 1 hour. Top with grated lemon rind. Canned shrimps may be used in place of crab.

Chrysanthemum and Radish *Sunomono*

6 ounces edible chrysanthemum flowers
⅓ pound *daikon* radish or turnip

Sauce
4 tablespoons vinegar
3 tablespoons sugar
1 teaspoon salt

Pull petals off flowers and boil in water that has had a little salt and vinegar added. Squeeze petals to press out water. Cut *daikon* into small rectangular slices and proceed as for the cucumber in the basic recipe. Mix sauce and pour over petals and *daikon*.

Shrimp-Cucumber-Celery *Sunomono*

2 cups peeled, deveined and boiled small shrimps
4 small or 2 medium-size cucumbers
Salt
1 piece of celery, or in Japan, *udo*
4 tablespoons vinegar
1 tablespoon sugar
Shredded fresh gingerroot

Put the boiled shrimps in the refrigerator to chill. Wash the cucumbers, but do not peel. Slice cucumbers into narrow matchlike strips. Sprinkle with salt, mix, and leave to stand for about 20 minutes to soften. Peel and string celery and cut into strips of the same size; soak celery in a bowl of ice water with a few drops of vinegar added.

When ready, stir, drain and squeeze out surplus liquid from the cucumber and celery without too much squashing. Combine remaining vinegar and a pinch of both salt and sugar to make a dressing. Add cucumber, celery and shrimps, mix, and serve in individual small bowls with a pinch of shredded gingerroot on top. Makes 4 servings.

In Japan *kabu* is a vegetable that one sees on the market in the fall and winter and it resembles a white beet. A small white turnip could be substituted. Dried persimmons are also a common sight on the Japanese market. They come in little straw coverings. Fresh persimmons are a common Japanese fruit on the market in the fall and not as sour as the persimmons one finds in America. If persimmons are not available, apple or pear could be substituted. Japanese cooking is an adventure, so one might as well have the fun of experimenting.

Kabu and Dried Persimmon *Sunomono*

6 small white turnips, sliced thin
1 teaspoon salt
Basic *sunomono* sauce (see page 70)
1 dried persimmon

Sprinkle the sliced turnips with salt. After about 15 minutes add the sauce. Slice up the dried persimmon. Roll up the pieces of persimmon in the slices of turnips or *kabu*. Cut both ends to make them about the same size. Makes 6 servings.

Sunomono in an Apple

Here is one of those very new versions of an old recipe. First introduced by some clever cook in a Japanese women's magazine, the idea of using the fruit itself for the bowl is very appealing to the Japanese people. I find that this recipe should be served with a spoon because the sauce penetrates the apple and it is delicious to dig out the apple meat itself.

72

Basic *sunomono* sauce (see page 70)
8 ounces *daikon* radish or turnip
8 ounces carrots
4 large apples
Lemon juice

Mix the ingredients for the sauce and toss finely cut strips of *daikon* and carrot in it. I again use the trusty potato peeler to get them as fine as possible. Let mixture stand in the refrigerator for about 3 hours. Just before serving, cut the top off the apple. Hollow it out. If you can save any good part of the apple, grate it and add it to the carrot and *daikon* mixture. Fill the apple with the mixture. A good precaution is to treat the apple with lemon juice so it doesn't discolor. Put the top back on the apple and serve. Not traditional but very good. Makes 4 servings.

Aemono   This is another way of dressing foods and it too could be thought of and served very much in the same way that we Westerners treat salads. You will also find some recipes for *aemono* among the *zensai* in the first section of this book because just a little dressed food in a small bowl is considered nice with saké at the beginning of the meal.

The Japanese way of eating is like the Japanese language: literal translations are often almost impossible. If the Western cook is going to try to find a relationship between the two ways of eating, it just isn't going to come off right. The same thing is true for the language. It can never be mastered if one insists on literal translations all the time. So when trying to cook Japanese, forget about soup first and dessert last or salad before or after the main course. Things like *aemono* can turn up at the beginning of a meal one day and near the end another day. It can be a side dish or part of a lunchbox and it will all be correctly Japanese.

When it comes to Japanese dressed foods, perhaps the vinegar dressing came first and then cooks tried other dressings for different flavors and textures. Seaweed, shellfish, chicken and various vegetables are cooked, cooled and dressed. New recipes are constantly being put together by creative cooks as anyone can see by reading the monthly Japanese women's magazines. It all proves that Japanese cooking is not standing still and the young housewife of to-day cooks in a different way from her mother or grandmother. The way the Japanese cook now is with lots of tradition and lots of freedom for experimentation.

Spinach Dressed with Sesame *Aemono*

This is one of the most delicious of Japanese gastronomical inventions. The sesame gives the spinach a truly wonderful, nutty flavor that everyone loves. When cooking the spinach, however, do it quickly and in very little water. No dressing is going to help the spinach if it is too soggy. This is a warning one never has to give a Japanese cook.

3 tablespoons sesame seeds
1 teaspoon sugar
2½ tablespoons *shoyu*
1 cup cooked spinach, coarsely chopped

Toast sesame seeds in a hot dry frypan for a few minutes, until they begin to jump. Pulverize the sesame seeds in a *suribachi* (mortar and pestle), reducing them to a paste. Add the sugar and *shoyu* and mix with the spinach. Serve hot or cold. Makes 4 servings.

Eggplant with Sesame Seeds *Aemono*

1½ pounds eggplant
4 tablespoons *shoyu*
2 tablespoons white sesame seeds
6 Japanese leeks, minced
1 red pepper, minced
1 teaspoon sugar

Wash the eggplant and cut lengthwise into slices. Place in a dish and sprinkle with half the *shoyu*. Steam until tender, drain off liquid, and let cool. Parch sesame seeds by heating them in a dry frying pan until they start jumping. Pound in a mortar, then add to leeks, pepper, remaining 2 tablespoons *shoyu* and the sugar; mix well.

Put a layer of eggplant slices in a serving dish, sprinkle with half the dressing, and repeat. Serve hot. Makes 4 servings.

Bean-Sprout Salad *Aemono*

½ pound bean sprouts
1½ tablespoons finely chopped Japanese long onions, both
    stalks and tops
2 tablespoons *shoyu*
1 tablespoon vegetable or sesame oil
2 tablespoons sesame seeds, toasted and crushed in a mortar
½ tablespoon sugar
¼ tablespoon garlic salt
Dash of cayenne

Cook sprouts in boiling, salted water for 2 to 3 minutes. Do not overcook. Quickly drain and chill. Combine all ingredients and chill. Drain again. Serve cold.

Japanese Asparagus *Aemono*

2 tablespoons vegetable oil
2 tablespoons sesame seeds
3 tablespoons vinegar
3 tablespoons sugar
1 teaspoon *shoyu*
1 pound fresh asparagus

Heat oil and in it cook sesame seeds until they are light brown. Remove from heat and let cool. Add vinegar, sugar and *shoyu* and blend well. Wash asparagus; break off and discard white ends. Steam asparagus for 4 to 5 minutes. Place in cold water immediately and cool thoroughly.

Drain asparagus and cut on the bias at ¾-inch intervals, leaving about 1 inch of tip. Pour sauce over all, turn carefully, and refrigerate until cold. Serve as a salad. Makes 4 to 6 small servings.

Dressed Clam and Long Onion *Aemono*

12 fresh clams
2 long onions
6 ounces white *miso* paste
2 tablespoons sugar
3 tablespoons saké
1½ tablespoons vinegar

Take clams out of shells, drain, and cut into convenient bite-size pieces. Plunge onions into boiling water for 1 second. Rinse with cold water. Cut off green tips, and shake or gently squeeze all water from inside. Cut into uniform 2-inch lengths. Mix *miso,* sugar and saké in a small pan; heat to boiling, stirring all the time. Remove from heat and transfer to a china bowl. Add vinegar to dressing; stir and chill. Arrange clams in individual small dishes, place onions on one side and *miso* dressing on the other. For correct consistency, the *miso* dressing should be approximately as thick as mayonnaise. Makes 6 servings.

Agemono—Fried Foods

Food is one of my favorite subjects. When talking to people who visit Japan, I get the feeling that if a vote could be taken on their favorite Japanese dish, *tempura* would win hands down. Everyone seems to enjoy the way the Japanese deep-fry fish, shellfish and vegetables. The secret to *tempura*'s taste is that the batter is made just before the frying takes place and the sauce is made quickly while the main ingredients are frying. As with other fine Japanese dishes, the ingredients must be the freshest.

Traditionally, the Japanese have not been a people overly fond of greasy foods and this can still be said to be true. Good *tempura* should never feel or taste greasy and therefore good *tempura* should never be allowed to stand. It should be eaten before it even begins to cool.

Eating this dish in a Japanese *tempura* restaurant can be great fun. The goodies are displayed and the customer can usually watch the cook deep-fry the food and bring it from pot to plate with one stroke of his chopsticks.

It is a perfect meal for a garden party or for a new kind of cookout. All that is needed is a gas burner to keep the cooking oil bubbling away. The fresh shrimps, fish and vegetables can be displayed in large flat baskets on the table and the cook can take orders for the foods the guest fancies. The guest can watch and in no time at all, the hot meal is on his or her plate. This is one bit of Japan that everyone seems to love and it is at home just about everywhere.

Other than *tempura*, there are several fried dishes that are part of Japanese cooking, made in ordinary shallow fry-pans. The housewife in Japan may cook up some of these tasty dishes from time to time, but on the evening she plans *tempura*, it is likely to be some kind of an occasion.

Tempura   To make *tempura* correctly, you must be just as insistent as a good Japanese cook that everything is fresh and freshly cooked. The batter must be made just before frying and the *tempura* must be served right away. Nothing should be left standing and even the sauce must be made quickly while the main ingredients are frying. The oil must be fresh. Sesame-seed oil combined with an equal amount of salad oil can be a very good combination for *tempura* frying, although almost any kind of vegetable oil can be used.

The oil should be at least 2 inches deep, preferably deeper, so that the ingredients are completely submerged. For a mixed *tempura* dish, begin by frying the most delicately flavored ingredients first. If you include onions, put them in last.

Tempura Batter

1 cup unsifted flour (all-purpose will do)
1 egg
1 cup cold water

Mix flour, egg and water together, beating it lightly without trying to make the mixture smooth. Never let the batter stand very long and don't worry if it has some lumps in it. Makes enough batter for 4 servings.

Prawns Cooked *Tempura* Style

Use large or medium-size prawns. Remove the heads and shells but leave the tails intact; remove the veins. Cut each prawn lengthwise in several places but not all the way through. Making little slits in the prawns will prevent shrinking in the frying process. Wipe off the water on the prawns so that the oil will not splatter.

Mix the batter; put 1 prawn at a time into it so that each is nicely coated with batter. Lower the prawn slowly into the boiling oil (350° F). When prawns are nicely browned, take them out and lay on a mesh or paper towel for a few seconds for the excess oil to drain off. Serve with a small dish of sauce for dipping.

Other Foods to Fry *Tempura* Style   Almost any kind of fish or raw vegetable can be fried *tempura* style. Suggested is any white fish, cuttlefish or shellfish. For vegetables, onion, carrots, green peppers, small eggplants, lotus root cut and sliced, and sweet potatoes, squash or pumpkin cut and sliced thin.

Sauce for *Tempura*-Style Fried Foods

Combine 1 cup basic *dashi*, 4 tablespoons *shoyu* and 4 table-spoons saké in a saucepan and bring to a boil. Let cook and put into individual dishes. Into this grate some *daikon* radish, or grate a turnip instead.

Chrysanthemum *Tempura*

When you want to do something different Chrysanthemum *Tempura* is the answer. It is a bit more work than the usual *tempura* but the flavor is great and the very thin *harusame* noodles make the flower design of your *tempura* very impressive. *Harusame* means spring rain; when you see the fine and light noodles, you will understand the name. This recipe makes a *tempura* that looks like a flower. It should be easy for you to make this dish very appealing to the eye as well as the taste. Make your chrysanthemum *tempura* and create an artistic work to bring to the table, but make it quick because these chrysanthemums should be eaten warm.

4 ounces peeled prawns
1 egg white
Pinch of salt
2 teaspoons flour
4 ounces *harusame* noodles
Oil for deep frying
3 or 4 chrysanthemum leaves
Grated radish
Grated gingerroot

Tempura sauce

Mince prawns, then pound in a mortar to reduce to a smooth paste. Add egg white, salt and flour; blend well. Shape 1-

inch-round patties from the paste. Cut *harusame* noodles into strips ½ to 2 inches long, depending on what length you like your flower petals. Press the prawn patties on one side only gently but firmly into the *harusame* strips. The idea is to preserve the round shape of the patties and, at the same time, to make them pick up as many "petals" as will stick. Deep-fry and drain patties. Arrange the newly cooked "chrysanthemums" in the form of a bouquet in a large dish and decorate with a few washed and dried chrysanthemum leaves. Serve with *tempura* sauce, grated *daikon* and grated gingerroot in separate dishes. Makes 4 servings.

Trout with Ginger

Japanese men love to fish; it seems to be a real pastime with them. Everytime you pass a brook, stream or river in Japan, there is sure to be someone there holding a fishing pole. It seems to be an exercise in Oriental patience because, except for remote places, inland waters are pretty well fished out by now.

But trout still swim in the mountain rivers and streams, and it is considered quite wonderful when a neighbor or relative brings over some freshly caught trout. If this happens in the U.S.A., not always, but very often the wife of the house is at a loss because cooking and cleaning a fish is not one of her favorite things. However, the Japanese housewife is delighted since she is very much at home with fish. The chances are the trout will end up being broiled—a simple good method—but it may end up in the frypan and come to the table spiced with that marvel of the Orient—ginger.

2 medium-size fresh trout
Flour
Oil for deep-frying
4 tablespoons *shoyu*
2 tablespoons saké
½ teaspoon sugar
4 slices of fresh gingerroot
2 Japanese long onions, cut into 1-inch sections
1 cup hot water
1 teaspoon salt

Dress the fish but do not remove head or tail. Score the sides and rub the fish on both sides with flour. Heat a pan and pour in 1½ inches of oil. When oil is very hot, lower the fish into it and fry for 1 minute on each side. Turn down the heat and continue to fry for 1 more minute on each side. Remove the fish and pour off the oil. Return the fish to the oily pan and add the *shoyu*, saké, sugar, gingerroot, long onions, water and salt. Cover the pan, turn up the heat, and cook quickly for 3 to 4 more minutes. Serve hot. Makes 4 servings.

There are several of what I call "new Japan recipes." They may not have been commonly served in Japanese homes in days gone by but Japanese cooking is not as pure today as it once was. Today it has more variety because women's magazines and T.V. stations employ creative people who go about thinking up new dishes to suit both the Japanese palate and what is available on the Japanese market. These are some of those recipes. They may come from untraditional sources, even from a cooking class, but the Japanese housewife serves them with pride and delight in her family's approval of her new type of cooking.

Fried Shrimp Balls

1 pound raw shrimps, shelled and deveined
1 slice of bacon, minced
6 mushrooms, fresh or dried
3 tablespoons fine-chopped long onions
1 teaspoon salt
¼ teaspoon ground ginger
¼ teaspoon pepper
1 tablespoon cornstarch
1 egg, slightly beaten
2 cups salad oil

Cut the raw shrimps into halves and put into a bowl with the minced bacon, mushrooms, onions, salt, ginger and pepper. If the mushrooms are dried, soak before cutting. Fresh or dried, cut them into very small pieces. Mix the cornstarch into the beaten egg and pour over. Mix with your hands and refrigerate until ready to cook. Just before your meal, heat salad oil until very hot. Drop shrimp mixture by the teaspoon into the hot oil. Cook, turning until shrimp balls turn pink, for about 2½ minutes. Remove balls from oil with slotted spoon; drain on paper towel. Serve hot and give each guest his own small dish in which to mix his sauce of hot mustard and *shoyu.* Makes 6 servings.

Tofu and Onions

This is another of those new-type Japanese recipes I saw made on a Japanese T.V. cooking program. I found that I liked it when I tried it, also that many of my Japanese house-wife friends were including it in their menus from time to time. Inexpensive and satisfying.

2 blocks *tofu,* about 20 ounces
2 tablespoons vegetable oil
2 Japanese long onions, sliced very thin
2 tablespoons *shoyu*
½ cup *dashi*

Press the *tofu* and cut into 1½-inch pieces. Remember that *tofu* has a large water content and can splatter, so be careful to press as much water out of the bean curd as you can before attempting the frying. Put oil in a frypan and when hot, add the *tofu.* Cook the *tofu* until it is nicely browned on both sides. Remove from the pan and add the onions. Cook them until they become golden, then return *tofu* to the pan. Cook for 1 minute. Pour off any excess oil. Add *shoyu* and *dashi* stock. Cover and cook over very low heat for about 6 minutes. Juice should be almost cooked away and the *tofu* should be flavored through. Serve with plain boiled rice. Makes 4 servings.

Deep-Fried *Tofu*

Cut a block (about 10 ounces) of *tofu* into 4 pieces. Pat dry with paper towel, making sure most of the water is out. If not, the hot oil may splatter. Put *tofu* pieces into hot oil and deep-fry for 3 to 4 minutes, until *tofu* is golden brown. Remove with a slotted spoon and drain. Serve in a small bowl or plate, garnished with grated gingerroot or grated long onion or leeks. Pass the *shoyu* to flavor it. Makes 2 small servings.

Chicken Balls with White Sesame Seeds

3 dried *shiitake* mushrooms
2 long onions
1 pound raw chicken, minced
1½ tablespoons *shoyu*
1½ tablespoons saké
Pinch of salt
1 teaspoon sugar
1 egg
Oil for frying
1½ teaspoons white sesame seeds

Soak the dried mushrooms in cold water to soften for 10 to 15 minutes. Remove stems and mince the mushroom caps very fine. Mince the onions just as fine and mix both with the chicken. Blend well with your hands. Season with *shoyu,* saké, salt and sugar. Stir in the egg and again mix well with hands. Shape into small balls by rolling between the palms of your hands. Fry in hot oil until golden brown. Drain on a paper towel. Either roll the chicken balls in the sesame seeds or arrange on a plate and sprinkle them with sesame seeds.

For those who want additional seasoning, serve individual small dishes with *shoyu* for dipping. Makes 6 servings.

Sweet Potatoes with Sesame Seeds

Cut up the potatoes as you would for french fried potatoes. Soak them in cold water, dry on paper towels, and fry in hot oil. Fry them very lightly, not letting them get too brown.

Put 1 cup sugar into ¾ cup water, bring to a slow boil, and let it cook over very low heat until it forms a syrup, about 8 to 10 minutes. Dip the hot sweet potatoes into the syrup, put on a plate, and sprinkle with black sesame seeds. Good hot or cold.

Tonkatsu (Pork Cutlet)

Maybe this dish is not considered a really traditional Japanese treat but it is very much a part of Japanese life today. The average housewife makes it often for her family and people enjoy it in neighborhood-type restaurants all over Japan. It is easy to make and even saved my life in a way when I was first trying to cook for a Japanese family. The basic way to fry the cutlet is much like frying a breaded pork chop. The difference is in the serving. The Japanese cut the cutlet into bit-size pieces and lay the pieces on a bed of finely cut cabbage. The pork is served along with a sauce called *Tonkatsu,* sauce which is much like the A.1. Sauce served in the U.S.A. It is part of the new cooking of Japan but by now is very popular. If you plan it as the main course, serve it on a separate plate, one smaller than a dinner plate. In Japan, this dish is served along with a small dish of pickles, hot miso soup and a bowl of steaming boiled rice.

Allow 1 pork cutlet for each person, usually cut from ¼ to ½ inch thick. Lay the cutlet out on a board and knead it with the handle of a large knife for a minute. Dust the cutlet with flour, salt and pepper. Heat oil in a frypan, dip the cutlet into beaten egg, roll in bread crumbs and fry, turning, until golden brown on each side and thoroughly cooked. While cutlet is cooking, put ¼ head of cabbage on the cutting board. With a very sharp knife cut down the side, making strips of cabbage as one does for coleslaw. Put the cabbage in cold water for a few minutes, shake out the water, and dry with a paper towel.

On each dish put a generous bed of the cabbage. Drain the cutlet on a paper towel to remove grease, cut it into bite-size pieces, pick it up carefully so it retains its cutlet shape and put it on the cabbage bed. The sauce is poured over the cutlet. Some people use just *shoyu* in place of the sauce. This dish can be made with the cutlets of other kinds of meat, such as chicken or veal, but it is most popularly made with pork in Japan.

Nabemono—Foods Cooked at the Table

To understand why cooking a meal at the table has become so popular in Japan, you have to know something about the life of the people. The Japanese house is usually small and not at all suited to cold weather. Often the houses are made of wood or paper with lots of door/windows. Totally suited architecturally for tropical climates, one wonders why the classic Japanese house is built even in areas that can be rather cold. Central heating is still not very common, except in the new buildings in the big cities, and even this development is fairly recent. The Japanese who works in a new-type heated office in downtown Tokyo, still usually goes home to small space heaters and the like.

To keep warm, the Japanese sit around a table called a *kotatsu*. It is probably an outgrowth of the open firepit that can still be found in country homes. The *kotatsu* is often built over a hole in the floor. One sits on the floor and there is a place to put one's legs down. A stove—nowadays more usually an electric heater—is in the hole and a quilt is fitted over the table. Another table top goes over the quilt to make it a cozy warm place to sit. You pull the quilt up around your lap and enjoy whatever activity one enjoys sitting at a table. People read, write, sew, play games and, of course, drink tea and eat meals there. What nicer way to eat than to have the pot of food cooking right on that very table!

The perfect table-top meal is something tasty cooked in one pot where everyone can take what he or she wants, putting the cooked food in smaller individual dishes. The pot is usually cooked on a charcoal brazier or, more commonly these days, a small portable gas burner. It all is reminiscent of the days gone by when people sat around the open fire and ate from the large kettle that hung over the flames.

There are many kinds of *nabe-ryori* dishes. *Sukiyaki* is by far the best known. It is an easy dish to duplicate anywhere in the world and the cooking pot can even be an electric fry-pan. The meat and vegetables are arranged on a plate and put into the pot in a certain order. They simmer in the savory sauce and the taste pleases just about everyone.

Nabemono offers an informal and friendly way to share a warm meal and is well worth trying. Using little Japanese bowls and chopsticks, you can serve this portable part of Japan for a delicious and different kind of dinner party. Of course, hot saké and friendly conversation is a *must* with this kind of meal.

Sukiyaki   No cookbook about Japanese food would be complete without a recipe for *sukiyaki.* Almost every family in Japan has its own and you too will find that you will develop one in time. Some people make the "sauce" beforehand but most families do not. Usually it is the man of the house who takes over the table-cooking of *sukiyaki* just as many Western men like to do the outdoor cooking. Often the cook just pours in *shoyu,* sugar, *mirin* and water according to his taste. For the beginner, it may be better to do the sauce first. The ingredients too may vary according to taste.

Sauce

1 cup water
½ cup *shoyu*
½ cup *mirin*
⅔ tablespoon sugar, or less (some like it sweeter than others)

Main Ingredients for Four

4 to 6 Japanese long onions
2 bundles of *shirataki* (arrowroot noodles, available in cans in Oriental stores), about 6 ounces
2 blocks *yakidofu* (*tofu* that has been browned on the outside), about 20 ounces
About 1½ pounds boneless beef, sliced thin

And any other vegetables you like. Suggestions are: bamboo shoots, *shiitake* mushrooms, spinach or edible chrysanthemum leaves.

Heat water, *shoyu, mirin* and sugar, bringing the sauce to a boil, and remove from heat. Cut onions at an angle into bite-size pieces. Wash *shirataki* and cut into 3-inch lengths. Cut bean curd *(yakidofu)* into squares and slice any other vegetables attractively. Arrange vegetables and meat on a large plate.

Heat the pan over the burner at table and melt a piece of fat in it, just enough to grease the bottom. Start the onions and other vegetables which take a long time to cook, keeping each kind in its own place in the pan. Place meat on top of the vegetables and pour some of the sauce over it all. Now carefully put in the *shirataki* and the *yakidofu*. Of course you don't put in everything at one time, but keep adding as needed. Add the greens at the very last.

Each portion should be eaten as it is cooked. There should be a raw egg (optional) in a small bowl at each person's place; the hot food is dipped into this egg, which has been well beaten with chopsticks. This operation may take a bit of getting used to but it is worth trying. The very hot *sukiyaki* sort of cooks the egg coating and this adds to the flavor.

Hot boiled rice is usually served with or after this dish. Many families add *udon* noodles or *mochi* rice cakes to the sauce near the end, instead of serving rice.

Shabu-Shabu

Another *nabemono* that has become a favorite with foreigners is called *shabu-shabu.* For this dish the ingredients are dipped into hot stock with chopsticks. The meat being swished back and forth as it cooks makes a noise that sounds to the Japanese ear like *"shabu-shabu."* Perhaps if this were a Western dish, it would be called "swish-swish." Let me repeat that every family and restaurant has its own favorite combination for this dish. The following are suggestions but a little experimenting will end up in developing your own favorite *shabu-shabu* combination.

1 head of Chinese cabbage, washed, drained and cut

¼ pound spinach, washed, drained and cut

½ pound bamboo shoots, washed and cut, or 1 can bamboo shoots

4 long onions or Japanese leeks, sliced diagonally as in the recipe for *sukiyaki* (regular round onions may be used if you like)

1 block of *tofu*, about 10 ounces, cut into cubes

6 cups basic *dashi* or stock as you prefer

Place vegetables and bean curd on a platter and arrange as attractively as possible. Pour about two thirds of the *dashi* or stock into your *nabe* pot which is set on a burner on the table. This could be an electric frypan. When very hot, add about one third of the vegetables, starting with the onions and bamboo shoots, spinach last. The rule is, the vegetables that take longer to cook go into the pot first. Place these ingredients carefully into the soup so that it all has some order, the onions in one place, the *tofu* in another and so on. The *tofu* breaks easily so be careful and put it in just before the last leafy vegetable.

People eat from the pot, dipping the food into the sauces which are in individual cups at each person's place. There is also a plate of meat on the table, about 1 pound for 4 people. Each person picks up a raw meat slice with his or her chopsticks and splashes it gently into the stock until it is cooked to the degree desired.

I suggest that you prepare two sauces as it is good to taste the difference in the flavor of the meat and vegetables dipped into different sauces. The following are some suggestions for *shabu-shabu* sauces.

Sauce 1

½ cup sesame seeds

1 cup *dashi*

½ cup *shoyu*

1 tablespoon vinegar

Cayenne

1 tablespoon oil

A touch of garlic (optional)

Toast the sesame seeds in a heavy dry pan, shaking until lightly browned. Grind to a paste in a mortar or whirl in a blender. Add *dashi, shoyu* and vinegar, stirring well. Add cayenne in judicious amounts to the oil, or use crushed dry red peppers if you prefer. If garlic is used, crush it to a purée and add to taste, or used powdered garlic. You can also have minced green onions and grated gingerroot for those who wish to add them.

Sauce 2

This is a simple, standard sauce and a must.

2 cups basic *dashi*
2 tablespoons *shoyu*
2 tablespoons *mirin*
Vinegar

Boil first 3 ingredients for a few minutes and let cool. Add vinegar to taste.

Sauce 3

Put soup from the pot into a small cup; let each person add the amount of *shoyu,* vinegar and garlic he likes. This is how the sauce is often made in Japanese homes. Also, grated gingerroot and finely minced long onions are on the table to be added to the sauce if one so desires.

Mizutaki

Boiled chicken *à la Japonaise* is a good meal for a winter evening. You can start this one in the kitchen if you like and take the chicken in the stock to the table to cook, or cook the chicken completely at the table, meanwhile enjoying an hour of saké drinking.

1 chicken, 2½ to 3 pounds
4 cups water
1 Japanese long onion
4 tablespoons *shoyu*
1 tablespoon *mirin*

1 long onion, finely chopped
3 tablespoons grated fresh gingerroot
Salt
Pepper
Lemon or lime, cut into quarters

Cut up the chicken smaller than you would for fried chicken. Don't remove the bones or skin. Put pieces in the water in your *nabe,* add 1 long onion, and bring to a boil. Let it boil away but remove any scum that forms. Let this cook for 40 to 50 minutes. Mix *shoyu* and *mirin.* Add to the soup and let cook a little longer. Let chicken simmer until everyone is ready to eat.

Put the chopped onion, gingerroot, salt, pepper and lemon or lime on the table. Spoon some soup into a little bowl at each place. When everything is ready, each person can take what he fancies and add it to the little bowl of soup.

Some people like to add a head of Chinese cabbage, washed and cut into quarters, to the *nabe* pot when the chicken is almost tender. This gives the soup a little different taste, but adds good flavor. Makes 4 servings.

Yosenabe

A kind of "everything in the pot" *nabemono*—a fish dish cooked at the table. It is sometimes thought of as a Japanese bouillabaisse, but the main difference is that this Japanese dish is never allowed to cook very long. It starts off with *dashi* stock as a base and the fish and carrots are already semicooked.

12 large raw shrimps, peeled and deveined
3 medium-size carrots, scraped
½ pound fillets of any white fish
12 Cherrystone clams, shucked
6 long onions or Japanese leeks
Greens—cabbage or spinach
3 cups basic *dashi*
1 piece of *konbu* (dried kelp)

Prepare shrimps. Cut the carrots into uniform pieces and cook in a little water until semitender. Take out, run under cool water, and put aside. Add the fish fillets to boiling water and simmer for 20 seconds. Drain and cool.

Arrange clams, shrimps, carrots, onions and fish on a large dish. Add some greens—cabbage or spinach.

When everyone is seated at the table, put the stock in the pot and add the *konbu* that has been washed and slit down the middle. Bring to a boil in the pot on the table. Let it boil for about 1 minute; remove the *konbu* with a slotted spoon and discard it. Now add the ingredients from the platter to the pot, the greens last.

Have each person take out what he wants with his chopsticks. Each will have a small bowl in front of him with a sauce made of 2 tablespoons saké and ½ cup *shoyu.* Let everyone put a spoonful of the soup into his own bowl of dipping sauce. Have red pepper and lemon or lime available on the table for those who like to add it to their sauces. Makes 6 servings.

Yudofu

This is truly Japanese "down home cooking," a very simple dish that is served often during the chilly months in homes all over Japan. It is nutritious, inexpensive and loved by the Japanese people.

4 blocks of *tofu*, about 40 ounces
1 or 2 long onions or leeks
1 medium-size knob of fresh gingerroot
Shoyu
1 cup bonito shavings
¼ cup saké
1 piece of *konbu,* long enough to cover the bottom of the pan

Cut *tofu* blocks into 18 cubes each. Slice onion thinly crosswise and grate the fresh gingerroot. Into a flat-bottomed saucepan place a cup filled with ⅓ cup *shoyu,* ¼ cup of the bonito shavings, and 1 tablespoon saké. The cup can be either the special cup available in Japan for making *yudofu* or just a wide-mouthed teacup or small bowl. Surround the cup with water in which the *konbu* is placed. Bring water to a boil and add part of the *tofu.* Bring water to a boil again. Add thoroughly heated *tofu* to the *shoyu* mixture in the cup. Let it stand in the hot marinade for about 1 minute, then transfer to individual dishes. Have the onion, gingerroot and the rest of the bonito shavings on another plate and sprinkle a bit of each of these things (as you desire) over the *tofu*. Eat *tofu* without·delay. Continue adding to the *shoyu* mixture as the *tofu* will absorb it quickly. Foreigners often like this without the bonito shavings. Makes 4 to 6 servings.

Teppan-yaki (Meat and Vegetables Cooked in a Skillet)

Though this is not, strictly speaking, a *nabemono,* it is still a very popular dish which is cooked and eaten around the table. Since almost all Japanese have a gas burner that can be placed in the middle of the table, a special evening of *teppan-yaki,* sometimes called *bata* (butter) *yaki,* can make a delightful family dinner. Again the ingredients are up to the cook, but here are some suggestions.

1 eggplant, cut into ½-inch crosswise slices
About 1 pound boneless beef, cut into ¼-inch slices
8 prawns (but perhaps the non-Japanese would prefer to
    keep it just a meat dish)
2 green peppers, quartered and seeded
4 large *shiitake* mushrooms
1 pound soybean sprouts
1¼ head of cabbage, cut into thin slices
Salad oil or butter

Soak the eggplant in cold water, drain, and dry well. Arrange the meat and prawns and vegetables on a large platter. Preheat skillet over high heat on table. Grease with salad oil or butter. Start with the meat, then continue with prawns and vegetables, letting the guests take what they want when ingredients are cooked.

There should be a dipping sauce; the easiest is diluted lemon juice with an equal amount of *shoyu.* This is put into a small bowl and the guest dips the meat, etc., into it. Makes 4 servings.

Tsukemono—Pickled Vegetables

It may sound like a simple pleasure, but anyone who has a fascination with food can have a wonderful time strolling around the basement area of most Japanese department stores. There is no end to the exotic goodies that are displayed so appealingly, and the pickle section is especially an eye treat. It may not be a real treat for the nose, but that is part of the fun.

The Japanese truly love their pickled vegetables and no Japanese meal would be complete without these *tsukemono* that go along with the rice at the end of a meal. The test of a good cook in Japan is just how good the pickles are, and making them used to be an art among Japanese housewives. Now, most city women pickle vegetables in salt every couple of days but the good, smelly, tasty *miso*-pickled foods are bought, probably in the basement of some department store. They are mostly pickled in rice bran and this is too much of a production for the city people these days.

In the old days when pickling was a common home occupation, there was a cask of salted bran that the housewife stirred thoroughly every day. Vegetables were put into the cask and allowed to stay for a long time, covered and pressed under a big stone. Semidried *daikon* radishes were and are a favorite pickle prepared this way. Still, in the country, a typical autumn sight in Japan is to see *daikon* hung outside the house, drying in the sun. These Japanese radishes will end up as pickles for sure.

Nowadays, however, the most common everyday pickles are the simple salt pickles. Chinese cabbage, cucumbers and small eggplants are the favorites. They are sprinkled liberally with salt, put into a crock, and pressed under a heavy lid or a big stone. Several hours to three days is the usual time of preparation in this manner. This is a simple type of pickle that can be made anywhere, even when Japanese food is being prepared far from Japan.

Small eggplants, the first of the season, are often pickled in *miso* paste with mustard and are considered a great treat. For this you must choose very small, young eggplants. With these and all pickles, the color as well as the taste is appreciated. Bright purple eggplants and bright green cucumbers show the skill of the cook.

Pickled Cold Eggplant

6 small eggplants
2 tablespoons salt
4 cups water
1 teaspoon *wasabi,* or hot mustard
3 tablespoons *shoyu*
3 tablespoons sugar
3 tablespoons *mirin*

Cut eggplants into fourths after slicing off the stems. Soak in water and salt for 1 to 2 hours to soften a bit. Drain and put into a crock or bowl. Mix all other ingredients and pour over eggplants. Turn or cover all the eggplants. Cover and refrigerate for about 3 hours, turning once or twice.

Pickled Cabbage

This is usually done with the Chinese cabbage called *hakusai* in Japanese. Cut a cabbage (about 2 pounds) lengthwise into quarters, wash, and drain. Put some salt into a stone jar and put in the Chinese cabbage in layers, sprinkling each layer with more salt (about 2 ounces salt in all). Press down flat, put a weight on top (a clean hard stone will do), and pour in water to fill the jar halfway. The pickled cabbage is ready when the water rises. Overnight is time enough in a warm room but they should not stand for longer than 3 days. Serve as a side dish with *shoyu* and rice.

Cucumber Pickles

Follow the cabbage recipe, using cucumbers in place of cabbages. The cucumbers should be washed and cut into 1-inch pieces but not peeled. Do, however, cut off and discard the ends.

Pickled Japanese *Daikon*

Soak the *daikon* radish in cold water for 10 to 15 minutes. Turnip may be substituted in the recipe. Rinse and dry well. Cut off the leaves and set aside. Chop *daikon* into small pieces and rub each with salt. Put the leaves in the bottom of the jar or jug. Slice and shred the *daikon* or turnip and put into the jar in layers. Sprinkle each layer with equal parts salt and rice bran if available; if not, coarse salt alone. Cover with a lid that can be pressed down by putting a weight on top and leave 5 to 6 hours. Before serving, press out excess liquid. Cucumbers may also be prepared this way.

Lotus Root in Vinegar Dressing

1 large lotus root
5 tablespoons vinegar
Salt
1 tablespoon sugar

Peel lotus root and at once put in water with 1 tablespoon vinegar added to it to prevent discoloration. Cut root lengthwise into halves, then into slices a little over ½ inch thick. Boil in water with a little vinegar until tender, and slice rather thin. Mix 4 tablespoons vinegar, pinch of salt and 1 tablespoon sugar, and blend well. Coat the lotus root slices with this dressing and leave to marinate in the refrigerator until ready, several hours.

Serve cold. For a special dish, put some of the drained lotus root in a small bowl, together with a few thin slices of smoked salmon.

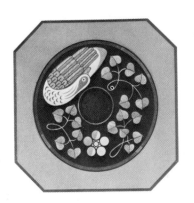

Misoshiru and *Suimono*—
Japanese Soups

You might say the Japanese are full of soup because they like to include it in just about every meal. Even a Japanese-style breakfast includes a piping hot bowl of *miso* soup. When I was growing up, my mother used to advise us children to eat our oatmeal so that it would stick to our ribs and give us energy to get us through the day. Perhaps this is how the Japanese mothers felt about a bowl of hearty *miso* soup to get their families on their way. In both countries, nowadays, toast, coffee and maybe dried cereal is more likely what is served every morning. However, weekends are often times for the treat of a good breakfast and in the Japanese sense, that is built around fresh, hot rice and *miso* soup.

Misoshiru, soybean-paste soup, can be and is served with lunch and dinner as well as breakfast. It has a basic *dashi* base and it can be made in a short time as it is not one of those soups that is improved by cooking a long time. It also doesn't take well to reheating so it should be made fresh. The soup is never allowed to boil after the *miso* is added. The other ingredients are cooked in the stock and the *miso* added just before serving. With this rule in mind, anyone should be able to make a good bowl of *misoshiru;* considering how hearty and nutritious this soup is, that is a plus.

The other really popular soup in Japan is called *suimono.* It is a clear soup with bits of fish, meat, vegetables or any number of other ingredients in it. It is easy to make once you learn the rules, and learning the rules tells you a lot about Japan. Eventually you can experiment and come up with combinations that will suit both Western and Japanese meals. This soup is usually served in individual, covered bowls, often lacquer—sometimes at the beginning of a formal meal, sometimes at the end and sometimes both. The soup is kept hot by a vacuum created when the lid is put on the bowl so before removing the lid, the bowl should be squeezed lightly to release the lid. It is perfectly correct to pick up the bowl and hold it in one hand when drinking Japanese soup.

There are three parts to Japanese clear soup. First, the base which is a stock and some protein. Second, the *tsuma* which translates into something like "accessory," and this is usually a vegetable or seaweed. Third is the *suikichi,* and this is harder to translate, but it is a kind of spice. A translation of the word means "sip mouth" and with a little imagination, you will get the idea. This is usually an ingredient that gives the soup a flavor of the season.

For the base in clear soup use basic *dashi* for the stock and a small piece of fish, shellfish, *kamaboko* (fish cake) or *tofu* as the protein. If you use chicken or eggs in place of the fish, it may taste better in chicken stock instead of *dashi* which is made from a fish base. For the *tsuma* or accessory, any kind of vegetable is fine—Japanese leeks or long onions sliced thin, bamboo shoots, carrots, seaweed, mushrooms, snow peas or even spinach.

For the *suikichi* use a little bit of something to give a subtle taste to the lips as the soup is drunk. The taste should remind one of the particular season, and that is part of the charm of Japanese cuisine.

Suggested Combinations

Dashi stock, small shrimps, Brussels sprouts sliced very thin, sliver of lemon

Vegetable *dashi,* sliced hard-cooked egg, asparagus or *warabi,* salted cherry blossom or a bit of *umeboshi* (pickled plum)

Chicken stock, *tofu, udo* or celery, mint leaf cut into strips

Chicken stock, bit of chicken meat, spinach, a sliver of fresh gingerroot

Dashi stock, sliced fish cake, snow peas, a bit of citron

Dashi stock, bits of white fish, Chinese cabbage cut very thin, lemon peel

Misoshiru   There are endless combinations from which to make *miso* soup. I'll include some definite recipes but the following also contains some information that could be useful when you set out to make your own variations, and that is what so much of Japanese cooking is all about. Basic rules with lots of freedom. If this were not true, Japanese dishes could be boring to prepare.

If you use vegetables such as turnip or potatoes, cut them into small cubes after they have been washed and peeled. Cook your vegetables (turnips, potatoes, carrots, *daikon* or finely chopped Japanese long onions) in the *dashi*. Dilute about 4 ounces of *miso* with a little of the *dashi*, and add the mixture to the soup. Heat to the boiling point but don't let it boil. Serve.

Other foods that are nice to add to *miso* soup are shredded cabbage, *abura-age* (fried bean curd), sliced into pieces, shredded mushrooms, chopped greens such as spinach and of course *tofu* (bean curd) that has been cubed. If *tofu* is added, it should be added carefully and last. It breaks easily and boiling makes it swell.

Cabbage *Miso* Soup

2 blocks of *abura-age* (fried bean curd), about 20 ounces
8 ounces shredded cabbage
5 ounces *miso* paste
5 cups *dashi*

Shred or slice the bean curd thin and mix with the raw cabbage that has also been shredded or sliced thin in similar strips. Dilute *miso* with a little *dashi*. Add the rest to the *dashi* soup that has already been brought to the boiling point. Lower the heat slightly, add bean curd and cabbage, and simmer for 2 minutes. Serve hot. Makes 4 servings.

Wakame or Seaweed *Miso* Soup

½ ounce dried *wakame* seaweed
4 cups *dashi*, basic or sardine
1 onion, thinly sliced
2 potatoes, peeled and cubed

Shoyu
Salt
4 ounces red *miso* paste

Soak the seaweed in cold water until soft, drain, cut into ½-inch squares. Bring *dashi* to a boil with onion and potatoes. Season with *shoyu* and salt, stir, and put in seaweed. As soon as soup heats and potatoes are cooked but not too soft, add 4 ounces red *miso*. Stir and simmer for another minute or two. Serve in individual bowls. Makes 4 servings.

Oyster *Miso* Soup

10 to 12 oysters
5 cups *dashi*
5 ounces *miso*
Pinch of red pepper

Wash and shell oysters. Wash again in very cold water, drain. Add to the *dashi* and bring to a boil. Lower heat, add *miso,* and simmer very gently for 1 minute. Season with a dash of pepper. Makes 4 servings.

Minced Prawn *Miso* Soup

8 ounces uncooked prawns, shelled and cleaned
4 cups *dashi*
5 ounces *miso*
1 block of *tofu,* about 10 ounces, cut into ½-inch cubes
Dash of ground ginger

Mince the prawns, put them into the *dashi,* and let them cook for a very few minutes. Make sure the heat is lowered, then add the *miso.* Add *tofu* cubes and the dash of ginger. Let soup simmer for only a few minutes after adding the *miso.* Makes 4 servings.

Pork *Miso* Soup

2 ounces Japanese leeks or long onions
2 ounces carrots, cut into strips
4 ounces potatoes, cut like the carrots
5 cups *dashi*
8 ounces boneless raw pork, thinly sliced
5 ounces *miso*

Cook the leeks, carrots and potatoes in the *dashi* until done but not too soft. Add the pork and cook for a few more minutes. Add *miso,* turn down the heat, and let simmer for 3 or 4 minutes. Serve, dividing the vegetables and meat evenly among the bowls. Makes 4 servings.

Suimono and Variations   In the beginning of this chapter I suggested some combinations for this basic Japanese clear soup. It is a piece of protein simmered in stock with a vegetable and a spice which is a very little bit of something to touch the lips with flavor. There are the classic clear soups served at fine Japanese meals, but there are other clear soups served in Japan that are heartier. An example of this is *ozoni,* which is the main dish served on New Year's morning. It is cooked on the stove, not on the table, and it is full of vegetables, fish or meat and the rice cake dumplings that make it proper for the New Year. There are other Japanese soups, heartier than the thin clear soups, which can serve as a main dish.

Clear *Matsutake* Soup

8 ounces raw skinned, boned chicken
Salt
2 medium-size or 1 large *matsutake* mushroom
Cornstarch
4 cups clear chicken stock
Dash of *shoyu*
4 pieces of lemon peel

Cut the chicken, allowing 2 pieces per portion. Sprinkle with salt and let stand while you trim and stem the mushrooms. Cut mushroom into small pieces, including the stem, allowing about the same amount of mushroom for each of the 4 portions this recipe makes. Dip the chicken lightly into cornstarch, then simmer in salted water until tender. Drain and set aside. Simmer the mushroom in the stock for about 3 minutes; drain but keep the stock. Add *shoyu* to stock.

Now put equal parts of chicken and mushroom in each bowl, add a piece of lemon peel, and pour the hot soup over it. Cover with lid and serve. Makes 4 servings.

Shrimp and *Daikon* Soup

6 ounces peeled shrimps, finely chopped
½ teaspoon sugar
Salt
1 egg, beaten
8 ounces *daikon,* cut into small cubes
2 tablespoons saké
8 *shiitake* mushrooms
2 ounces spinach
4 cups basic *dashi* or stock
Shoyu

Combine shrimps, sugar, a small pinch of salt and beaten egg, then mix thoroughly. Sprinkle *daikon* cubes with saké and salt and add to shrimps. Cook mushrooms and spinach together in a very little stock. Bring rest of stock to a boil, add all other ingredients, season with *shoyu* to taste, and simmer until done. Put a portion of shrimp mixture, 2 mushrooms and a spoonful of spinach in each bowl, pour the hot soup over them, cover with a lid, and serve at once. Turnips or potatoes may be substituted for *daikon.* Makes 4 servings.

Japanese Chicken Noodle Soup

2 ounces *udon* (Japanese noodles)
Salt
4 ounces boneless raw breast of chicken, sliced
3 cups chicken stock
2 tablespoons *shoyu*
12 dried *shiitake* mushrooms
Dashi or stock for cooking vegetables
4 pieces of lemon rind

Boil *udon* in salted water and drain. Put chicken in a pan with 1 cup boiling water and simmer until tender. Add *udon,* chicken stock and *shoyu.* Soak dried mushrooms in water for 10 minutes to soften, remove stems, then simmer in *dashi* for cooking vegetables for 10 minutes. Don't use the chicken stock as the mushrooms will give it too strong a flavor. Drain mushrooms and add to the *udon.* Season with salt to taste and heat through. Divide chicken, mushrooms and *udon* among the bowls, pour the soup over them, float a piece of lemon rind on each bowl, and cover with a lid. Serves four.

Egg and *Fu* Soup

2 ounces spinach
2 eggs
4 cups *dashi*
½ teaspoon salt
¼ teaspoon *shoyu*
2 tablespoons *arare-fu* (wheat gluten)

Cook the spinach in very little salted boiling water for 3 to 4 minutes. Drain and chop. Beat eggs, add *dashi,* salt and *shoyu,* and simmer over very low heat for 3 to 5 minutes. Add *fu* 1 minute before serving. Makes 4 servings.

Japanese Egg-Drop Soup

4 cups *dashi* or chicken stock
1½ teaspoons salt
1 teaspoon saké
2 teaspoons *shoyu*
2 eggs
1 piece of gingerroot, thinly sliced
4 parsley sprigs

Bring *dashi* or stock to a boil. Blend salt, saké and *shoyu.* Add to *dashi* and simmer for a few minutes. Beat eggs into a froth and, using a perforated spoon, float them on the surface of the soup which should be kept simmering over very low heat. Do not just pour in the egg mixture as this would sink it below the surface. Do it gently. Then pour soup into individual bowls, add a slice of gingerroot to each, and float a small piece of parsley if you like. Makes 4 servings.

Tofu Soup

4 cups *dashi* or stock
1 long onion or leek, chopped very fine
1½ teaspoons salt
½ tablespoon *shoyu*
2 ounces spinach, chopped
1 block of *tofu,* about 10 ounces, diced
1 teaspoon finely chopped gingerroot (optional)

Bring *dashi* to a boil with onion, salt and *shoyu.* Add spinach. Let simmer for 5 minutes. Add *tofu,* sprinkle with ginger, and simmer for 1 more minute. Serve at once. Makes 4 servings.

Pork Soup with Vegetables

12 dried mushrooms
1 carrot
4 ounces spinach
5 cups *dashi*
Salt
2 teaspoons *shoyu*
8 ounces raw or cooked pork, cut into thin slices
1 Japanese long onion, chopped fine

Cut the mushrooms into thin slices. Cut carrot into 1-inch pieces and slice lengthwise into matchstick shapes. Cut washed spinach into pieces about 1 inch long. Heat the *dashi;* add salt and *shoyu.* When it boils add the pork, carrot, mushrooms and onion. Let simmer for about 10 minutes. Add the spinach and let soup simmer for 1 more minute. Serve hot. A dash of ground ginger is sometimes added. The recipe can also be made with fish in place of the pork. Makes 4 servings.

Ozoni

This is a traditional New Year's soup but it doesn't have to be New Year's morning to enjoy it. Like so many Japanese traditional dishes, this varies from area to area and family to family. The following is an *ozoni* that is sure to please the Western palate.

2 cups water
4 cups chicken stock
8 ounces raw chicken breast
1 *daikon* radish, or 2 carrots
2 taro roots, peeled (optional)
⅓ cake of *kamaboko,* about 2 ounces
6 ounces spinach, cooked
Shoyu
Lemon or orange slice
8 pieces of *mochi* (rice cakes)

Add water to the chicken stock and bring to a slow boil. Add the chicken, cut into bite-size pieces; cut *daikon* and taro to match the chicken pieces. Cut *kamaboko* into slices and cooked spinach into 1-inch lengths; add all this to the soup. Season with *shoyu* to taste. Cut lemon or orange slice into small pieces. Toast *mochi* until it begins to color golden brown. Into each bowl put 1 *mochi* cake, a piece of chicken, a slice of *kamaboko* and a few pieces of each vegetable. Fill up the bowl with the hot broth and add a piece of lemon or orange. Makes 4 servings.

Gohan—Rice and Variations

Tiny Japan grows far more rice than its large population cares to eat today but that hasn't always been the case. For centuries it was a struggle, and being a rice farmer was hardly a rewarding occupation. Today they are among some of the richest Japanese, and the government-controlled warehouses bulge. Ever since the end of the war, the government has guaranteed the rice farmer higher and higher prices for his rice.

Both people and the press complain about the problem of expensive rice rotting in the warehouses. It is certainly not a perfect system; still, today just about all the Japanese can afford to buy rice, if they want. The problem, as bad as it is, is still an improvement over the days when there wasn't enough rice for the people to eat.

Bread has become increasingly popular since the end of the war, but the Japanese people eat it more for convenience than preference. It requires no cooking and therefore has become desirable for breakfast and sometimes lunch. Actually, most Japanese would rather have rice three times a day, if cooking it wasn't so much trouble.

The Japanese are very creative with their rice dishes. They love good plain boiled rice but they cook red *sekihan* for happy occasions; they cook rice in a gruel for babies and people who are ill; they take it in little bundles and balls on picnics; they put it in lunchboxes; they even make cakes and sweets from it. Rice plays an important role in the life, economy and diet of the Japanese. As a result, a cook is very much judged by his or her skill in preparing it.

There are many festivals in Japan to celebrate rice-planting and rice-harvesting. The Emperor himself plants some rice each year in a symbolic gesture as part of one of the many rice ceremonies. The day that is set aside for the first eating of the new rice is something like Thanksgiving and it is a national holiday. Japan is still truly a rice culture.

Variations   Besides plain rice, the recipe for which I gave you in the "explanations" section at the beginning of this book, the Japanese housewife delights in cooking rice with the first of the season vegetables such as bamboo shoots in the spring or mushrooms in the autumn. Sometimes a meal in a pot is made, so to speak, when the rice is cooked with bits of fish or meat and maybe vegetables too. Rice is prepared with a great many things in Japan to give it many different flavors—it is even sometimes cooked with tea.

Mushroom Rice

3½ cups uncooked rice
2 to 3 ounces mushrooms
2 tablespoons *shoyu*
1 teaspoon salt
¼ teaspoon saké
4 cups water

Wash rice thoroughly and let stand for 1 hour. Wash mushrooms lightly with a soft cloth. These are usually *matsutake* mushrooms or pine mushrooms, but almost any kind will do. Cut off root and slice stems and caps into thin pieces. Put rice, *shoyu,* salt and saké into the water. Place the mushrooms on top of the rice. Cook in the usual way. When done let stand for 10 minutes or more. Mix and serve in individual bowls. Some people like to add *konbu* seaweed to the water, making a soup of it before adding the rice. Makes 4 servings.

Bamboo Rice

3½ cups uncooked rice
About ¼ pound fresh bamboo shoots, or 1 can bamboo
   shoots
1 tablespoon *shoyu*
1 teaspoon salt
1½ teaspoons *mirin*
4 cups water

Wash rice thoroughly. Cut fresh bamboo shoots into small thin pieces and boil in water for 30 minutes or so. Put rice, bamboo shoots, *shoyu,* salt, *mirin* and water into a *kama* or rice cooker and cook in the usual way. If you are new at it and cooking it in an ordinary pot, set it on the stove, bring to a boil, and keep over very high heat until the rice begins to bubble over. Reduce heat to low, cook for 20 minutes, turn off heat, and allow rice to stand for 10 minutes. Serve in individual bowls. It is very important to let rice stand covered for 10 minutes after taking it off the heat, to let it settle.

Kuri Gohan (Chestnut Rice)

3½ cups uncooked rice
24 small chestnuts (fewer if they are large)
1 tablespoon *shoyu*
1 teaspoon salt
½ teaspoon saké
4 cups water

Wash rice thoroughly. Shell chestnuts, peel off the brown skin, cut each chestnut into halves, and leave to soak in water to soften. Put rice, chestnuts, *shoyu,* salt, saké and water into your rice cooker or pot and cook as you usually cook rice. Follow earlier directions for plain rice. Serve in individual bowls.

Tori Meshi (Chicken-Vegetable Rice)

3 cups uncooked rice
4¾ cups water
4 chicken fillets
4 cups chicken stock
3 *shiitake* mushrooms
2 pieces of bamboo shoots
½ medium-size carrot

Sauce
1 cup of stock that chicken has been boiled in
1 teaspoon sugar
1 teaspoon *shoyu*
½ teaspoon salt
Dash of ginger juice

Cook rice as usual. Cook the fillets in the 4 cups of chicken stock for about 10 minutes. Remove the fillets, cool and cut into strips. Soak the *shiitake* mushrooms until soft and cut into strips. Cut the bamboo shoots and carrot in strips of a similar size.

Mix the ingredients for the sauce, combine in a saucepan and add the chicken and vegetable strips. Cook over low heat until vegetables are just underdone, about 5 minutes. Add the chicken, vegetables and sauce to the 4 cups of chicken stock and bring the mixture to a boil.

Fill 4 rice or soup bowls about two thirds full of rice. Arrange one fourth of the vegetable and meat mixture on top of each bowl. Just before serving, add the very hot soup, to which you have added the dash of ginger juice. Makes 4 servings.

Crab and Steamed Rice

2 cups glutinous rice
4 cups water
4 medium-size crabs
1 tablespoon *shoyu*
1 tablespoon salad oil
½ teaspoon sugar
½ teaspoon salt

Marinade
¼ cup saké
2 tablespoons *shoyu*
1 slice of gingerroot, finely chopped
2 long onions or Japanese leeks, finely chopped

Bring the rice to a boil in 4 cups water, turn down the heat, and simmer for about 30 minutes or until water is absorbed; set aside. Marinate the crabs in the saké mixture for 30 minutes, turning them occasionally. Season the rice with *shoyu*, oil, sugar and salt and put it in a deep, heatproof serving bowl. Arrange the crabs on the rice and pour the marinade over all. Put the dish on a rack in a steaming vessel, being careful that the water does not overflow into the bowl. Steam for 1½ hours. Serve in the bowl very hot. Makes 4 servings.

Ochazuke (Tea over Rice)   An easy and common meal in Japan. It consists of rice in a rice bowl, something to flavor it with and hot green tea poured over it. Many end their meal with *ochazuke* and many make it a quick meal when there is neither time nor desire to bother with real cooking. *Ochazuke* is flavored with many things and "instant" flavoring for this quick dish is sold in Japan. Usually *nori* seaweed and sesame seeds are a must. Sometimes bits of pickled gingerroot or pickled radish are also put on the rice, topped with sesame seeds (white or black) and tiny strips of *nori.* Hot tea is poured over this for a homey dish of *ochazuke.*

Sekihan (Red Rice)   Rice with red beans is a kind of happy rice, red being a color for congratulations in Japan. It is served on festive occasions such as New Year's, for weddings or even birthdays. When a baby has its first birthday, sometimes the happy parents of the healthy child will send boxes of *sekihan* to neighbors and relatives. This is a way of sharing a happy occasion; a graduation or building a new house could call for some red rice too. To make it one needs *mochi* rice, which is a glutinous rice.

3½ cups *mochi* (glutinous) rice
½ cup *azuki* (dried red beans)
5 cups water
2 tablespoons black sesame seeds
½ tablespoon salt

Wash rice and leave covered with water overnight. Wash the red beans and also allow to stand in water. Then boil the beans in 5 cups of water, stirring constantly; drain, but keep the water. Cook the rice as usual, using the red bean liquid for more water if necessary. As soon as the rice bubbles over, add cooked beans; mix and continue to simmer until rice is done. Serve hot or cold in individual bowls. Mix sesame seeds with salt, parch dry in a pan, and sprinkle over the rice. Makes 6 servings.

Onigiri, Rice Balls and Rice Triangles   These are some of the ways rice is taken along on picnics, in lunchboxes or whenever and wherever it is more convenient to have cold rice. A good *onigiri* is eaten with much appreciation in Japan.

Rice Balls and Triangles

2 cups rice
2 tablespoons black sesame seeds

Cook rice as usual and allow to cool. Parch the sesame seeds in an ungreased heated pan until they begin to jump and then pound them in a mortar. Shape the rice into small balls or triangles with your hands. Moisten your hands with lightly salted water to do so. When you have the shape you desire, roll it in the sesame seeds. Makes 8 to 10 small servings.

Onigiri

Follow the above directions, only roll the rice into a larger ball, about the size of a duck egg. Country people often make these rice balls as large as a baseball but city people prefer them smaller. Bore a deep hole in the middle with your finger and put in either a pickled plum or bits of pickled mushrooms. Shape it back into a perfect ball again and wrap it with a piece of *nori* seaweed that has been made crisp by holding it over a flame.

Gohei Mochi

Another rice ball recipe, this one is said to have become famous in the days when samurai walked about with swords swinging. It appears that the samurai made this mochi from cold rice balls while resting from a battle. The rice balls were said to have been roasted at the end of a sword.

⅓ cup sesame seeds
1 ounce sugar
2 ounces *miso*
3 cups boiled rice (1 cup cooked rice makes 5 rice balls)

Put sesame seeds in a mortar and grind. Add sugar and *miso* to the mortar and pound into a paste. Add some water and put contents in a pan over heat; pound into a sauce. Cook rice softer than usual and, while it is still hot, pound to make it sticky. Not too much though, since it shouldn't be like *omochi* rice cakes. Divide into 3 parts and make 5 balls out of each third of the rice. Put the balls on a skewer and roast over a fire or on a wire net. Usually there are 2 balls to a skewer, depending on the size. Now dip the roasted rice balls into the *miso* sesame sauce and roast again. For a variation, try grinding grated gingerroot into the *miso.* This makes great cookout fare.

Sushi *Sushi* rice is in a class by itself. It is a slightly sweet-sour rice and it is served in many different ways. *Sushi* shops are very popular all over Japan and having *sushi* ordered in is usually something done only for guests or on special occasions. When *sushi* is made at home, the cook expects lots of compliments and usually gets them. Everyone seems to like rice *sushi*-style. Besides *sushi* rice rolled in seaweed, it is most often made into little finger shapes and placed under strips of the freshest raw fish, shellfish or perhaps Japanese omelet.

Sushi-Gohan (Rice for *Sushi*)

10 cups uncooked rice
12 cups water
1 cup mild, white vinegar (rice vinegar is ideal)
2½ tablespoons salt
2 tablespoons sugar

Wash rice carefully 3 hours before cooking. Pour into a draining basket and let sit. Bring water to a boil; add rice, keeping the water boiling. Turn down heat when the rice begins to bubble over; simmer for 10 minutes. This should give the rice the required consistency. Transfer to a large shallow pan or bowl and fan until cool. Japanese use a paper fan to cool the cooked rice. Mix the other ingredients, pour over the cooled rice, and move the rice around until it is well coated and tastes sort of sweet-and-sour.

Norimaki (*Sushi* Rice Rolled in Seaweed)

By tradition, *norimaki* requires 6 layers of various ingredients, each prepared separately before rolling. This is too much of a production for home cooking so the recipe that follows is only for cucumber- or mushroom-filled *sushi.*

Let 6 big dried mushrooms soak in lukewarm water for 15 minutes to soften. Remove stems and cut into strips. Put 5 tablespoons stock or *dashi* into a pan. Add 1 tablespoon sugar and 1 tablespoon *shoyu* and cook the mushrooms in this mixture. When the liquid is reduced, take out the mushrooms and put them on a paper towel to drain.

Now wash 4 long thin cucumbers. Cut off the ends and slice them the long way into very thin strips.

Take a sheet of *nori* seaweed and hold it over direct heat to make it crisp. Lay it on one of those bamboo mats called *sudare* and spread an even layer of the *sushi* rice on it. Make the rice come up to the edge of the *nori* sheet on the sides but leave about ½ inch of uncovered seaweed on the top and bottom to allow for essential overlapping. You can, if you want, spread the rice with a little grated *wasabi* or Japanese hot horseradish. Place your filling, either of cucumbers or mushrooms, down the middle in a thin line and roll everything up in the *sudare,* being careful to make sure that the seaweed forms a tight casing around the filling. The secret is to make a good tight roll. Remove the *sudare,* and repeat. Cut each roll into 8 or 9 pieces with a sharp knife.

The filling can also be made of eggs, fish eggs, ground fish, spinach, dried gourd shavings and many other things.

Chirashi Zushi

Enough boiled rice to serve 4 people
Salt, sugar, vinegar
4 ounces snow peas
1 cup *dashi*
½ cup *shoyu*
¼ cup saké
2 carrots
2-inch piece of lotus root (optional)
2 eggs
4 dried *shiitake* mushrooms
2 ounces red pickled gingerroot
12 small cooked shrimps, peeled and deveined

Put the cooled rice in a large pan and season with 2 teaspoons salt, 2 tablespoons sugar and 2½ tablespoons vinegar.

Mix well. Boil the snow peas for a minute in salted water, but do not overcook. Drain and season with ¼ teaspoon salt and ½ teaspoon sugar. Mix them so they are well coated and put aside. Make a sauce to cook the other things in. This recipe is a simplified method but it works if you follow instructions. Cooking everything in the same sauce, but not at the same time, makes sense and if you cook the foods with the stronger flavors last, there is no problem. Cook mushrooms last as they have the strongest flavor.

Mix ½ package of instant *dashi* (or make it from the beginning: see page 22) in 1 cup boiling water. Add about ½ cup *shoyu*, ¼ cup saké and ½ cup sugar. Bring to a boil and turn off heat. Slice or shred carrots, and cook in the sauce gently until tender. Remove with a slotted spoon. Peel and chop lotus root and let simmer gently in the sauce until root turns whitish. Remove and drain.

Now take a tablespoon of that sauce and put it in a bowl. Add the eggs and beat well with a fork. Grease a square pan lightly and fry a very thin, pancakelike omelet. Remove, lay out omelet on a cutting board, and cut into strips.

Soak the mushrooms until soft, remove stems, and shred caps. Cook in the sauce for about 2 minutes. Cut gingerroot into thinnest possible slivers. Mix rice with shrimps, carrots, mushrooms, lotus root, snow peas and egg strips. Divide into 4 individual dishes or put it all on a platter. Either way it should be arranged in a decorative manner, reserving the fine strips of red ginger to sprinkle on top.

Donburi (Another Way to Serve Rice)   A *donburi* bowl is larger than a rice bowl and it has a cover. This is a very popular meal-in-a-bowl in Japan and the combinations that go over the rice are up to the cook. Small portions of meat, fish, bean curd and vegetables are cooked, then beaten eggs are mixed in and the whole cooked like an unstirred omelet. The omelet is put over the hot rice and the lid is put back on the bowl. *Donburi* is almost always served with a side dish of various Japanese pickles.

Sukiyaki Donburi

1 block of *tofu*, about 10 ounces
2 tablespoons oil
4 onions, chopped
2 ounces carrot, minced
2 ounces *shiitake* mushrooms, cut into strips
4 ounces boneless raw beef, cut into strips
3 tablespoons *shoyu*
Pinch of salt
1 tablespoon sugar
2 eggs, beaten
2 cups freshly cooked rice

Squeeze out excess liquid from the bean curd. Heat oil in a frypan and put in the onions, carrot and mushrooms. Fry, adding beef when the onions begin to look golden. Cook for about 2 minutes, adding the bean curd last. Stir gently to blend; season with *shoyu*, salt and sugar, then mix. Remove from heat. Fan and stir to cool for a few minutes. Now put back on the heat with the eggs mixed in. Cook until the eggs begin to set. Fill individual bowls with steaming rice. Cut the large omelet into 4 parts and put 1 part gently over each bowl of rice. Cover bowls. Makes 4 servings.

Oyako Donburi

This is another popular meal-in-a-bowl. The name means mother-and-child since both the chicken and the egg are used. Despite whatever associations this name might have for Westerners, the result is delicious.

8 ounces dried mushrooms
6 tablespoons *mirin*
6 tablespoons *shoyu*
4 tablespoons sugar
1 cup *dashi*
8 ounces chicken, thinly sliced
4 ounces onions, thinly sliced
6 cups freshly cooked rice
6 eggs
2 sheets of *nori* seaweed

Soak mushrooms in lukewarm water for 15 minutes. Drain, remove stems, and cut caps into narrow strips. Bring *mirin* to a boil, simmer for a couple of minutes to thicken slightly, then add *shoyu*, suagar and *dashi*. Bring to a boil; add chicken, mushrooms and onions. Cook gently until chicken is done. Season to taste, stir once, and divide mixture into 6 portions. Fill individual *donburi* bowls with steaming hot rice and cover with lids. Taking the portions of chicken and mushroom mixture one at a time, heat in a small frypan. Beat an egg lightly, pour over mixture in pan. Before the egg sets completely, remove mixture from the pan and arrange it on top of a bowl of rice. Hold *nori* seaweed over the fire for a moment to make it crisp; crush with your hands, sprinkle part of it over egg, and replace lid on the bowl at once. Repeat this procedure with the other 5 portions and serve. Makes 6 servings.

Menrui—Japanese Noodles: *Soba* and *Udon*

People who visit Japan for the first time are often very surprised to find that the Japanese are very fond of their pasta. Any Japanese city or town has many types of noodle stands and restaurants, and their grocery shops carry a wide variety of dry and precooked noodles.

Soba are thin noodles made of buckwheat flour. They are very popular and are eaten any time of the day. So, rice is not the only grain eaten in Japan. The country people tell me that polished white rice was considered a luxury to the poor folk until some years ago. There was a time when other grains, millet and buckwheat, were their everyday fare.

Buckwheat came to Japan in about the eighth century through Korea from China. In the Nara and Heian periods (about a thousand years ago) buckwheat was used as sort of emergency food. It was made into a gruel or mixed with rice to stretch the meager rice ration.

Then, during the seventeenth century, a Korean monk had the idea of mixing the buckwheat flour with wheat flour to give it more body. With the extra body the wheat flour gave the buckwheat, it could be worked into a dough and made into noodles. These were called *sobakiri* or cut *soba* or *soba* noodles.

Soba became a very popular dish during the Edo period (seventeenth to nineteenth centuries), and stands selling this fast food sprang up everywhere within a very short period. The best *soba* is still called *ni-hachi* or two-eight *soba*, meaning two parts wheat flour to eight parts buckwheat flour. It is still a great Japanese favorite during all seasons.

Other noodles in Japan are *udon* which are like fat spaghetti. *Somen,* on the other hand, is a very thin wheat vermicelli. *Harusame* is a very thin noodle made from soybean powder. *Harusame* means spring rain, so it is not too difficult to visualize what these look like. *Chasoba* is a pretty green-colored noodle made of buckwheat and green tea.

Shirataki is also considered a noodle by some but it is actually a jellylike food made from tuberous roots and gelatin. This is a low-calorie noodle and can be very useful in planning interesting meals for a reducing diet.

Japanese people seem to have a passion for eating out and everyone in Japan seems to love noodles. This may be because the average Japanese home is rather small and the average Japanese life-style is rushed. Consequently, the Japanese child brought up in the city has had more experience eating out than his American city kid counterpart. In today's Japan, Sunday night is the popular evening for the family to go out to the local restaurant. Modern housewifes seem to be very pleased if their husbands consent to such a family outing, even if it is only to the local, low-cost noodle shop.

Like other things in Japan, noodles too have their seasons. Noodles cooked in hot broth are good anytime but are particularly good when the weather is cool or cold. Summer is a favorite time for cold noodles, and these are made even more refreshing sometimes when ice cubes are added to the dipping sauce.

In rural places in Japan, like Niigata, mid-August is the time to remember and honor one's ancestors and the Itoh house is no exception. Not only is the Buddhist altar dusted and polished, but offerings of flowers and food to please the ancestors are placed on the altar. Of course, many packages of *somen*, a noodle that is served in the summer, are cut, tied neatly and placed in pretty small plates on the altar to please any family ghost that just might return to remember the good things he had in life. To the Japanese, *soba* is a definite part of the good things in life.

Basic *Soba* Sauce

4 cups *dashi* stock
¼ cup *shoyu*
¼ cup *mirin*

Boil the ingredients for a few minutes and let the sauce cool. Chill sauce in the refrigerator if it will be used for cold *soba*. Some people like to add grated gingerroot and *togarashi* (powdered red pepper) to the sauce. To please everyone's taste, it is good to have these things available on the table and let everyone doctor up the sauce as he likes.

Summer *Soba*

Cook *soba* noodles until almost soft. Drain and plunge into cold water. Place the noodles on a plate or flat basket and garnish with several pieces of *nori* seaweed, cut into very thin strips. Place the chilled sauce in separate small bowls or Japanese *soba* cups and add very thin slivers of long onion.

Crab *Soba*

Here is a delicious *soba* dish that a Japanese housewife might prepare to please her family for a Sunday lunch.

3 dried *shiitake* mushrooms
3 tablespoons *shoyu*
1 teaspoon *mirin*
1½ teaspoons sugar
2 eggs
Oil for frying omelets
2 cucumbers
4 ounces red pickled gingerroot
2 spring onions
6½ ounces canned crab meat
White sesame seeds to garnish

Soak, stem, and shred mushrooms. Cook for a few minutes in the sauce made from the *shoyu, mirin* and sugar. When mushrooms are well-coated and soft, put aside and chill. Beat eggs with the sauce left over from the mushrooms. Oil a pan lightly (a square frying pan is best) and fry very thin, pancakelike omelets. Cut into strips. Wash the cucumbers but do not peel. Cut into very thin slices. Cut gingerroot into thinnest possible slivers Cut the onions into very thin slices.

Flake the crab and arrange side by side with the other ingredients, all well chilled. This looks best on a glass plate for a summer meal. Garnish with white sesame seeds and serve along with the summer *soba.* Eat crab and vegetables along with the noodles and dip them into the sauce. Makes 4 servings.

Tempura Soba

Batter: 4 ounces unsifted flour, 1 egg, and 1 cup cold water
Enough oil for frying
2 large prawns for each person
Cooked *soba* noodles
Soba sauce
Long onions, cut up

Mix flour, egg and water together, whisking lightly, without trying to make the mixture smooth. A few lumps won't matter as *tempura* batter is intended to be used immediately after mixing. Never let it stand.

Heat the oil slowly. Prepare prawns, dip into batter, and fry. Drain on a paper towel. Fill a bowl with cooked *soba* noodles, and pour *soba* sauce over the noodles. Garnish with cut-up long onions and place the fried prawns on top. This can be served cold, but is very good served hot too.

Fried *Soba*

8 ounces *soba* noodles
4 teaspoons oil
1 cup of ¼-inch squares of *hakusai* (Chinese cabbage)
6 teaspoons *shoyu*
Dash of *togarashi* or red pepper
2 long onions, cut very, very thin

Boil *soba* until tender, drain, and rinse to prevent stickiness. Combine oil and cabbage and cook until cabbage is wilted. Add *soba, shoyu* and *togarashi,* and stir gently until heated through. Add onions and serve piping hot.

Bean Curd with *Udon*

12 ounces *udon* or similar noodles
6 cups *dashi*
1½ tablespoons saké
4 tablespoons *shoyu*
1 tablespoon sugar
4 blocks of *abura-age* (fried bean curd), about 40 ounces
1 teaspoon salt
3 long onions or Japanese leeks

Boil the *udon* noodles in water until soft. Rinse in cold water and drain. Make a mixture of ½ cup of the *dashi,* the saké, 2 tablespoons of the *shoyu* and the sugar. Cut bean curd across on an angle to make 2 triangles from each square. Cook in the mixture for a few minutes. Take out with a perforated spoon and drain on a paper towel. Boil the rest of the *dashi* which has been seasoned with the remaining *shoyu* and salt. Remove from heat, add *udon,* cover, and leave to heat thoroughly. Put *udon* in individual bowls, place bean curd on top, garnish with Japanese onions or leeks that have been chopped very thin, pour the soup over all, and cover with a lid. Very good served with a small side dish of Japanese pickles.

Kudamono—Fruit for the End of the Meal

The Japanese meal doesn't build up to a luxurious dessert as meals often do in other countries. Traditionally, ovens were not part of the Japanese life-style and a cake was a dumpling or jelly-type sweet that was served to be eaten with tea. There were and are many kinds of cookies and crackers but none of these things was planned as part of a main meal. Rather they were something to go along with tea. Since the Japanese serve tea many, many times during a day, a sweet cake can easily be served to a guest when he first enters a home or a restaurant. Much to the Westerner's surprise, this is sometimes served before dinner.

Fruit comes to the Japanese table many times a day too but it is more often treated as a dessert, especially in recent years. It is the Western influence that brought the idea of a bit of sweet after a meal. After the final bowl of rice that ends a Japanese meal something super-sweet such as chocolate would just never do, but fruit and things made from fruit seem now to be an accepted idea of what a dessert should be. Very sensible, these Japanese.

The Japanese, however, treat their fruit differently. It is almost always peeled before eating. Even the skins of grapes are not eaten and this may seem rather terrible to the Westerner but the Japanese are just as shocked to see Western people eat the skins of fruit which the Japanese consider too tough and unpalatable.

The fruit stores overflow in Japan with the fruits of the season. Strawberries enjoy a long season, starting late in February and lasting through very early summer. The summer brings plums, peaches and various types of melons. A bit later grapes and figs are plentiful and then the *nashi* or Japanese pear that is so delectable. Later there are persimmons and all winter *mikan* or mandarin oranges are on every housewife's shopping list.

Mikan Surprise

In Japan, *mikan* or mandarin orange is as much a part of life as are Mt. Fuji or cherry blossoms. From fall through early spring, this excellent fruit is abundant, inexpensive and superdelicious in Japan. Most Japanese homes buy them by the box because everyone eats so many of them.

This recipe can be made with navel oranges, tangerines or ordinary mandarin oranges. It makes a thoroughly delightful snack or dessert anywhere, anytime.

To make *Mikan* Surprise, you must take the top off 4 large tangerines or oranges by cutting about three quarters of the way up. It is wise to make a little notch so that you will be able to replace the cap exactly.

Take out the pulp carefully. Remove all membrane and pith. You can now use 1 box (3 ounces) of orange-flavored gelatin and prepare as directed on the box, adding some of the orange pulp, or you can do it the real Japanese way, using 4 leaves of *kanten* gelatin. This is more trouble because it must be melted in 1 cup of water and orange juice to which 4 ounces of sugar must be added.

Whichever system you use, when the mixture begins to gel, add pieces of the fruit and spoon carefully into the orange cup. Place the cap back on and chill.

Stewed Fresh Figs

In Japan when figs begin to appear on the market, just about every home has a large jar of stewed figs in the refrigerator. They are served to guests in some of the little bowls that are so plentiful and pretty in Japan.

For 12 fresh figs, bring to a boil ¾ cup sugar and 1½ cups water. Add peeled figs to boiling syrup and simmer gently for 5 to 10 minutes. Cool and refrigerate.

Persimmon Cups

More and more the round, sweet, Far East version of the persimmon is becoming available around the world. Firm and beautiful, the fruit can be cut out with a melon-ball cutter and it makes a most attractive dessert. It takes about 1½ persimmons for 1 cup to be filled with round evenly cut balls. The persimmon is cut three quarters of the way up and hollowed out. A teaspoon of *mirin* put in the bottom of the cup, just before the persimmon balls are put into it, gives it a different but delightful flavor. Chill before serving.

Strawberries in Snow

2 tablespoons unflavored gelatin
2 cups water
1½ cups sugar
8 strawberries
2 egg whites
Small amount of grated lemon rind
1 tablespoon lemon juice

In a double boiler, soften gelatin in 1 cup water for a few minutes, add sugar, and cook until gelatin and sugar are completely dissolved. Wash and stem strawberries and wipe dry. Wet a mold or individual cups. Beat egg whites in a bowl until stiff. Gradually beat in gelatin mixture, grated lemon rind and juice. Keep on beating until slightly thickened. Pour into a rectangular mold or cup. Insert strawberries and refrigerate until set. When set and chilled, take out of mold, cut into squares, and serve. Makes 8 small servings.

Grapefruit Japanese

Though hardly native to Japan, grapefruit has become fairly popular in recent years. It once was extraordinarily expensive but that has changed and a half-grapefruit is something that appears on many Japanese tables nowadays. Sometimes the housewife who has been reading homemaking magazines will try to impress her guests by pouring a teaspoon of hubby's best brandy over it..

Deep-Fried Fruit

I learned this from the Japanese television cooking class and find it delightful. Many of my Japanese friends like it too. A neighbor likes to make this dish with bananas and calls it "banana *tempura.*" I prefer to make it with *mikan* or orange sections and call it *mikan* fritters. Whatever the name, it is equally good.

6 fresh *mikan* or mandarin oranges (navel oranges can also be used)
1 cup sugar
2 cups all-purpose flour
⅛ teaspoon salt
2 tablespoons melted butter
1 egg, separated
Vegetable fat for deep-frying

Prepare the oranges, removing all pith. Boil sugar and 1 cup of water together for 5 minutes. Cool to warm. Soak *mikan* or orange segments in syrup for at least 1 hour. Sift together the flour and salt, add the melted butter, beaten egg yolk and about 1 cup lukewarm water. Mix to make a light and smooth batter. Leave batter at room temperature for 1 hour. When ready to cook and serve, beat egg white stiff and fold into the batter. Heat fat. Drain segments of the *mikan* or orange and dip into the batter. Fry in deep hot fat until lightly brown. Drain on a paper towel and serve immediately.

If using bananas, peel and cut into 8 pieces. Brush with a bit of lemon juice and put into the syrup as in above recipe, leaving banana pieces to soak up the syrup a shorter time than you needed for the orange segments.

Chestnuts and Cream

Again one of those new-style recipes made with chestnuts, an old Japanese favorite.

Soak chestnuts overnight in enough water to cover. Peel and soak in fresh water. Boil in enough water to cover until soft. Rinse in cold water, drain, and dry on a paper towel.

When dry, press through a sieve. To serve, use a tablespoon to scoop up the purée and pile a small mountain of the chestnut grains on a small pretty dish. Top with sweetened whipped cream.

Candied Chestnuts

24 shelled chestnuts
10 ounces sugar

Soak chestnuts overnight in enough water to cover. Peel and soak in fresh water for several hours. Boil in 2 cups of water until soft. Add sugar and continue to simmer until done. Turn chestnuts in the syrup from time to time so that they are well coated. Remove the pan from the heat and leave chestnuts in the syrup until cool.

These chestnuts are eaten like candy, or just one is served on a dish as a dessert or, during the meal, with other foods such as fish or meat for the taste variety that is so important in Japanese cuisine.

Nomimono—Beverages

Nomimono are things to drink and one can't go into the drinking habits of the Japanese without first and foremost talking about tea. Just about every Japanese man, woman and child consumes a great amount of tea every day.

Tea in Japanese is *ocha.* Everyone knows that both the name *cha* and the brew itself came from China, but still Japanese folklore credits one of its own Buddhist saints with the miracle of making the tea plant grow and discovering what to do with it.

According to the story there once was a very devout monk named Daruma who sat on a mountain, determined to spend his years in constant meditation. He had a very difficult time staying awake but managed well enough for some five years. Finally his eyelids grew so heavy that, in spite of his determination, they closed. Rigorously, he forcefully ripped his eyelids from his eyes and flung them on the ground. On the very spot where the eyelids landed, a lovely green-leaved, white-flowered plant grew. He soon discovered that the plant leaves made a wonderful brew that was so stimulating that he could continue his meditation without again falling asleep.

This story may sound a bit fanciful but the Japanese do seriously credit the monk Daruma with introducing tea to Japan early in the sixth century.

In ancient times tea was just for the very upper classes and the clergy. It was expensive and considered a kind of health drink. Today it is drunk by everyone on any and every occasion.

Actually Japanese tea has many varieties but the two most common are *sencha* and *bancha. Sencha* is a green tea made of very tender leaves and there are many subcategories of *sen-*

cha. Some of the very fine ones can be quite expensive. *Bancha,* on the other hand, is considered a less fine tea since it is made of less tender leaves, with even some stems included. It brews a brown tea that is very tasty, and visitors to Japan often prefer it over the finer *sencha.*

Other teas worth mentioning are *genmaicha* which is a tea blend mixed with bits of popped brown rice. This has a very rich good flavor and is often served in Japanese homes. In the summer, *mugicha* is considered the best tea to drink. It is made from roasted, unpolished barley and is sold in bags. This is thought by many to be a true health drink. The housewife roasts the barley in a dry frying pan and then brews it in boiling water. It is strained, put in a bottle and refrigerated, and usually served cold. Almost all Japanese homes have chilled *mugicha* ready to serve on a hot day. Many a practical Japanese housewife employs a used whiskey bottle to store the *mugicha* in. Since tea can be mistaken for whiskey, as far as color is concerned, it puzzled me at first as to why so many Japanese homes had a bottle of whiskey in their refrigerators. I very soon learned, however, about this tea which is so delicious served cold and is so worth the trouble of preparing it. Like so many other things in Japan *mugicha* is made even easier since it can now be brought in large tea bags. The summer of 1978 saw this development; no doubt, in some years to come, the old-fashioned way of brewing *mugicha* may be forgotten.

The bright-green powdered tea that is served in the Japanese tea ceremony is called *matcha.* The Japanese tea ceremony is too sophisticated a subject to cover in a few words but I will say that *matcha* is always made from the very highest quality tea. Most non-Japanese find the taste too bitter at first, but the beauty of the ceremony enchants many of us. It is a very pleasant experience and the philosophy behind it has influenced countless Japanese things including Japanese manners and certainly Japanese cuisine. This powdered green tea too originally came from China where it was one of the earliest forms of tea. However, nowadays, few Chinese have ever tasted it.

The black tea that is favored in the West is called *kocha* and has gained considerable popularity in recent years. It is drunk in clear imitation of the West, being served in Western-style teacups with handles, along with sugar, lemon or milk. It is mostly served for guests in Japanese homes and in Western-style restaurants and coffeehouses. Many Japanese, especially women, often prefer black tea to coffee.

This doesn't mean that coffee is not popular in Japan, because in spite of its very high price it is, especially with the younger generation. There are coffee shops all over Japan but coffee or black tea have nothing to do with Japanese meals. Japanese tea is the traditional drink along with or after a Japanese meal.

Nowadays, many Japanese are getting into the habit of making their green tea with the tea bags commercially available. Still, the making of tea is such a simple and pleasant homely ritual that I feel it will be some time before the majority of Japanese housewives give it up.

To make Japanese green tea, buy it at Oriental food stores. You can usually tell how good the grade is by the price. The Japanese put the tea leaves directly into the teapot and often do not use a strainer when pouring, since a few leaves in the teacup are considered only natural and proper.

For a teapot serving, say 4 cups, you would use about 1 tablespoon of green tea. Also remember that the Japanese do not usually use boiling water. The water is poured into the pot just before it boils. And, of course, green tea is drunk absolutely plain—without milk, lemon or sugar.

Ume-shu **(Plum Wine)**   A delightful wine for all seasons is the Japanese wine made of plums which is called *ume-shu*. Served chilled in the heat of the summer or at room temperature at other times, it is a sweet delightful drink. It is made in just about all Japanese homes, usually in June, when the rainy season knocks down so many unripe green plums from the numerous Japanese plum trees. And it is served with pride.

To make *ume-shu* you will need about 8 pounds of unripe small green plums. Also 1½ bottles of *shochu* or white liquor, available in shops that sell Oriental food, but vodka could be substituted. You will also need 4 pounds of sugar. Rock sugar is commonly used in Japan but ordinary ground sugar works just as well.

Wash the plums and make sure you dry each one well.

Put them in a deep jar and add the sugar. Pour in the *shochu* or white liquor and cover the jar lightly; foil with a rubber band will do. Put the jar in a dark cool place and let the wine age for at least a month. In the summer serve it over ice, in the winter at room temperature; spring or fall, any way you fancy. The plums are delicious; after the wine is ready, put them into a compote and try them topped with whipped cream— not Japanese style, but great.

Saké   Just about every country in the world has its very own brew and Japan has a truly special one, called saké. It is a light white wine, made from the ever-important rice, and can be appreciated by almost everyone.

The fine clear water that is so plentiful in mountainous Japan has much to do with the good taste of this drink. The best saké is made with pure water and top-quality, newly harvested rice. The skill of making good saké is no problem because the Japanese have had lots of practice. It is even mentioned in the *Kojiki* or Record of Ancient Matters, which was written in 712. If saké was an ancient matter in 712, it is a superancient brew by now.

Delicious saké deserves every bit of its long popularity. It is a drink that has woven itself into the very patterns of Japanese life; it is part of almost all Japanese ceremonies both happy and sad. Drinking from the same saké cup is even part of the traditional wedding ceremony, and almost every Japanese occasion calls for the sharing of a cup.

When drinking a toast in Japan the word to say is *kampai* and it is heard all over Japan many times every day. As I said before, the Japanese love to party and drinking saké is a very important part of partying. It is the favorite drink and hot saké is a superfavorite drink. It is particularly good in autumn, winter and spring when the winds blow and homes can be pretty chilly.

Saké is warmed in small, and often beautiful, china or pottery bottles. The bottle is carefully placed in a kettle of warm water and warmed to body temperature, which is called *hitohada* in Japanese. This is about 100° F., or perhaps a little more, assuming that all taking part in the party are warmhearted people. It is then served in tiny cups. Part of the fun is keeping the saké cups of those sitting near you filled. A good geisha, or even a good host, hostess or neighbor sitting next to you at a saké drinking party, never allows one to fill his own saké cup. There is a great deal of unspoken friendship employed in filling a saké cup.

As an American girl transplanted, let me here inject one small personal note about saké. The very first time I arrived in Niigata as the blue-eyed bride of a Japanese man, I went from the train station to my new home and found all the village out waiting to see me. Through the big gates of the ancient homestead I went and found many of the townspeople gathered in a large *tatami* room, waiting to welcome me. My first lesson in being a wife in Japan was a strong suggestion that I go around with a warm saké bottle to each guest. Since everyone was sitting on the floor, I had to move around on my knees, stop before each guest, pour some hot saké for them, and simply smile and bow—knowing not one word of the language at that time. Every one of those town folk handed me back his saké cup in a return gesture and filled it for me to drink. Though I had been horrified at sharing all the local germs, in a very short time, both germs and I were tipsy—both from all the rice wine and from the happiness of these people's sharing all their warmth with a stranger.

In Japan there are many, many different brands of saké but they generally conform to a grading that any buyer or drinker can fully appreciate. The best saké is called *tokkyu* and that means special class—the very best. *Ikkyu*, first class, is therefore really the second best; it is considered excellent. *Nikyu*, second-class saké, may be third class but it is still popular and enjoyed by many. Because standards are so high in the age-old art of saké-making, one can drink even third-class saké and still feel confident that a perfectly good drink is being enjoyed.

In a class all by itself is *jizake*, a saké brewed with its own local flavor in many rural areas of Japan. It is not always available in Japanese cities and certainly not in stores outside of Japan, but you should know it exists. When you travel in Japan, it can be a special treat in areas such as Niigata where the local rice and the local water is considered excellent.

When talking about drinks in Japan, *amazaké* should also be mentioned. This is made of a glutinous rice turned into a kind of gruel with malt added. After it is distilled, it is a mild, sweet drink and can be very good on a very cold night, especially served warm with a bit of grated ginger.

Actually *amazaké* is commonly made from the wastes of real saké-making, and so is that other beverage called *sho-chu*. Nothing fancy about this drink, but it is still widely drunk by Japanese who like to get a glow inexpensively. Sometimes this is drunk mixed with *mirin,* the rather sweet cooking saké that so many of the recipes in this book have called for.

Last but not least, let me tell you about *otoso*. It may not be the best-quality saké but it is happy saké to me because the New Year is started off with its taste. For many people in Japan, waking up on the very first day of the New Year, the thing that first touches their lips is *otoso*. It is a sweet saké spiced with the flavors of many things such as beans, the rind of the mandarin orange and ash. Japanese believe that drinking it on New Year's morning means extended life and a new year free of problems.

On the first morning of the New Year, many a Japanese family gathers, immaculately clean and now dressed in the finest clothes. The head of the household greets everyone, wishing good fortune to each of them—the members of his family. *Otoso* is then served in a beautifully decorated pot and even the children sip the sweet purifying beverage.

I personally found this one of the loveliest customs in Japan. Because it seems so graceful and so disciplined to me, it is a custom I intend to keep on New Year's mornings, wherever I may go.

There are many good things from Japan that can enrich our Western lives. I sincerely hope that this book will touch your life with a few.

INDEX

About the Author

Joan Itoh knows about Japanese cooking the real way. As the wife of a Japanese, living with a Japanese family, she had to learn it. Though she now lives in Tokyo, she was then living—the only foreigner within miles—in Somi, on the rice-growing plains of Niigata in Japan's far northern snow-country. It was there that she also first started writing about Japanese food—her weekly columns for *The Japan Times* and her first book, *Rice-Paddy Gourmet.* As her interest in and knowledge of Japanese cooking grew, she saw that there was as yet no book of Japanese cooking as it really is today. Contemporary Japanese cooking, not self-conscious country cooking, not "classic" Japanese cuisine, but what the Japanese are really eating—this is what came to interest her most and the result is *Japanese Cooking Now.* She knows her subject as do few other foreigners, having lived in Japan now for almost fifteen years, and she intends to stay, always learning more about the wide and wonderful world of Japanese food.